THE WORLD HOLIDAY AND TIME ZONE GUIDE 1999

TERRI MORRISON
JOYCE HAYDEN
WAYNE A. CONAWAY

GETCUSTOMS.COM

The World Holiday and Time Zone Guide 1999

ISBN 1-886284-47-4
Library of Congress Catalog Card Number 98-83118
First Edition
ABCDEFGHIJK

Published by
Chandler House Press
335 Chandler Street
Worcester, MA 01602
USA

President Lawrence J. Abramoff

Publisher/Editor-in-Chief Richard J. Staron

Director of Retail Sales and Marketing Claire Cousineau Smith

Editorial/Production Manager Jennifer J. Goguen

Book Design Bookmakers

Cover Design Marshall Henrichs

Chandler House Press books are available at special discounts for bulk purchases. For more information about how to arrange such purchases, please contact Chandler House Press, 335 Chandler Street, Worcester, MA 01602, or call (800) 642-6657, or fax (508) 756-9425, or find us on the World Wide Web at www.tatnuck.com.

Chandler House Press books are distributed to the trade by
National Book Network, Inc.
4720 Boston Way
Lanham, MD 20706
(800) 462-6420

To Alexandra Lelia and Monica Clarissa,
Who make every day a holiday.
—*Terri Morrison*

To Stella Ferrari Conaway and Wayne Elias Conaway
Yesterday, today, and tomorrow.
—*Wayne Anthony Conaway*

May our diverse joys bring singular Peace and Truth.
To Theresa, Carl, Patrick, and Kevin,
The joys of my life.
—*Joyce Hayden*

CONTENTS

INTRODUCTION

Getting Through Customs (known on the Internet as Getcustoms.com) is pleased to present The 1999 World Holiday and Time Zone Guide to 77 countries. We hope that it will be of use to everyone who travels internationally or conducts business across national boundaries. It may be of use to those who host visitors from these countries as well.

Getting Through Customs (GTC) wishes to thank the many officials from around the world who have provided the data in this Guide. GTC has made every effort to ensure that the data is correct. However, governments change—and official holidays are declared by governments. This book also includes tips on doing business in each of these countries. The information in these tips can be dynamic too; a sales or negotiating technique which works today can become passé tomorrow. Consequently, GTC assumes no responsibility for the dates or information presented in this Guide.

Getting Through Customs and Chandler House Press intend to make the publication of this Guide an annual event. We appreciate your suggestions and comments. The study of intercultural communication represents a lifelong interest for the authors. By way of continuing that research, the authors invite your comments. Whether your own experience confirms or diverges from the data in this book, we would like to hear from you. Your comments may be sent to Getting Through Customs at:

Phone: (610) 725-1040
Fax: (610) 725-1074

E-Mail Address: TerriMorrison@getcustoms.com

Mailing Address: 638 West Lancaster Avenue, 2nd Floor
Malvern, PA 19355 USA

or visit our Website at: http://www.getcustoms.com

USING THIS GUIDE

Each year, thousands of international executives and travelers look for information on holidays and time differences around the globe. This compact guide offers an official list of holidays in 77 countries, along with valuable cultural tips for doing business in each. We hope this data facilitates schedules for multinational travelers, and entices many to experience exotic festivals in all parts of the world.

The first section shows time zones, holidays, and cultural tips for 77 countries, listed alphabetically.

The next section contains holidays in the United States of America, listed by state.

The next section is a day-to-day calendar for 1999 which shows every day that will be observed as an official holiday—anywhere in our list of 77 countries.

Following the calendar is a time difference table that helps you determine what time it is in each country, and any potential overlap of business hours.

Also included is an appendix compiled by Transparency International. Transparency International is dedicated to drawing attention to corruption around the world. As part of this effort, this Berlin-based organization has compiled the Corruption Perceptions Index (CPI). Corruption is difficult to document—by its nature, it tends to remain hidden. Transparency International notes that the CPI quantifies the *perception of corruption*, using a number of sources for each country. The countries are ranked from least corrupt (#1, Denmark) to most corrupt.

Finally, there is a section about Getting Through Customs—the authors of this book.

We welcome your comments for future editions of this guide, and can be reached through our Website at http://www.getcustoms.com or (610) 725-1040 or by fax (610) 725-1074.

1999

January

S	M	T	W	T	F	S
					1	2
3	4	5	6	7	8	9
10	11	12	13	14	15	16
17	18	19	20	21	22	23
24	25	26	27	28	29	30
31						

February

S	M	T	W	T	F	S
	1	2	3	4	5	6
7	8	9	10	11	12	13
14	15	16	17	18	19	20
21	22	23	24	25	26	27
28						

March

S	M	T	W	T	F	S
	1	2	3	4	5	6
7	8	9	10	11	12	13
14	15	16	17	18	19	20
21	22	23	24	25	26	27
28	29	30	31			

April

S	M	T	W	T	F	S
				1	2	3
4	5	6	7	8	9	10
11	12	13	14	15	16	17
18	19	20	21	22	23	24
25	26	27	28	29	30	

May

S	M	T	W	T	F	S
						1
2	3	4	5	6	7	8
9	10	11	12	13	14	15
16	17	18	19	20	21	22
23	24	25	26	27	28	29
30	31					

June

S	M	T	W	T	F	S
		1	2	3	4	5
6	7	8	9	10	11	12
13	14	15	16	17	18	19
20	21	22	23	24	25	26
27	28	29	30			

July

S	M	T	W	T	F	S
				1	2	3
4	5	6	7	8	9	10
11	12	13	14	15	16	17
18	19	20	21	22	23	24
25	26	27	28	29	30	31

August

S	M	T	W	T	F	S
1	2	3	4	5	6	7
8	9	10	11	12	13	14
15	16	17	18	19	20	21
22	23	24	25	26	27	28
29	30	31				

September

S	M	T	W	T	F	S
			1	2	3	4
5	6	7	8	9	10	11
12	13	14	15	16	17	18
19	20	21	22	23	24	25
26	27	28	29	30		

October

S	M	T	W	T	F	S
					1	2
3	4	5	6	7	8	9
10	11	12	13	14	15	16
17	18	19	20	21	22	23
24	25	26	27	28	29	30
31						

November

S	M	T	W	T	F	S
	1	2	3	4	5	6
7	8	9	10	11	12	13
14	15	16	17	18	19	20
21	22	23	24	25	26	27
28	29	30				

December

S	M	T	W	T	F	S
			1	2	3	4
5	6	7	8	9	10	11
12	13	14	15	16	17	18
19	20	21	22	23	24	25
26	27	28	29	30	31	

2000

January

S	M	T	W	T	F	S
						1
2	3	4	5	6	7	8
9	10	11	12	13	14	15
16	17	18	19	20	21	22
23	24	25	26	27	28	29
30	31					

February

S	M	T	W	T	F	S
		1	2	3	4	5
6	7	8	9	10	11	12
13	14	15	16	17	18	19
20	21	22	23	24	25	26
27	28	29				

March

S	M	T	W	T	F	S
			1	2	3	4
5	6	7	8	9	10	11
12	13	14	15	16	17	18
19	20	21	22	23	24	25
26	27	28	29	30	31	

April

S	M	T	W	T	F	S
						1
2	3	4	5	6	7	8
9	10	11	12	13	14	15
16	17	18	19	20	21	22
23	24	25	26	27	28	29
30						

May

S	M	T	W	T	F	S
	1	2	3	4	5	6
7	8	9	10	11	12	13
14	15	16	17	18	19	20
21	22	23	24	25	26	27
28	29	30	31			

June

S	M	T	W	T	F	S
				1	2	3
4	5	6	7	8	9	10
11	12	13	14	15	16	17
18	19	20	21	22	23	24
25	26	27	28	29	30	

July

S	M	T	W	T	F	S
						1
2	3	4	5	6	7	8
9	10	11	12	13	14	15
16	17	18	19	20	21	22
23	24	25	26	27	28	29
30	31					

August

S	M	T	W	T	F	S
		1	2	3	4	5
6	7	8	9	10	11	12
13	14	15	16	17	18	19
20	21	22	23	24	25	26
27	28	29	30	31		

September

S	M	T	W	T	F	S
					1	2
3	4	5	6	7	8	9
10	11	12	13	14	15	16
17	18	19	20	21	22	23
24	25	26	27	28	29	30

October

S	M	T	W	T	F	S
1	2	3	4	5	6	7
8	9	10	11	12	13	14
15	16	17	18	19	20	21
22	23	24	25	26	27	28
29	30	31				

November

S	M	T	W	T	F	S
			1	2	3	4
5	6	7	8	9	10	11
12	13	14	15	16	17	18
19	20	21	22	23	24	25
26	27	28	29	30		

December

S	M	T	W	T	F	S
					1	2
3	4	5	6	7	8	9
10	11	12	13	14	15	16
17	18	19	20	21	22	23
24	25	26	27	28	29	30
31						

Time Zones around the World

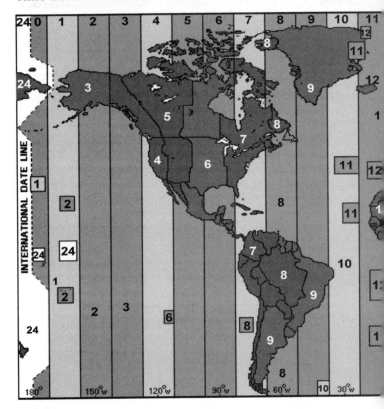

Adelaide **21**	Delaware **7**	Irkutsk **20**
Anadyr **1**	Denver **5**	Jakarta **19**
Anchorage **2**	Edmonton **5**	Johannesburg **14**
Athens **14**	Frankfurt **13**	Karachi **17**
Beijing **20**	Geneva **13**	La Paz **8**
Brussels **13**	Gorki **16**	Lagos **13**
Buenos Aires **9**	Halifax **8**	Lima **7**
Cairo **14**	Helsinki **14**	London **12**
Canary Islands **12**	Ho Chi Minh City **19**	Los Angeles **4**
Caracas **8**	Hong Kong **20**	Madrid **13**
Chicago **6**	Honolulu **2**	Magadan **23**
Dawsen **4**	Houston **6**	Manila **20**

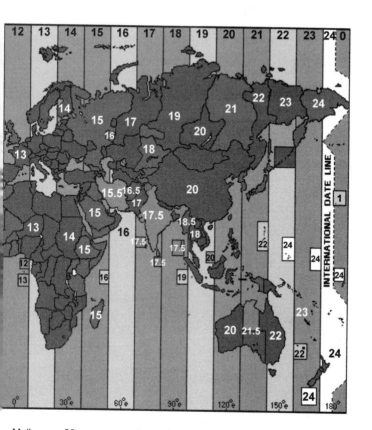

Melbourne **22**

Mexico City **6**

Milan **13**

Moscow **15**

Mumbai **17½**

New Delhi **17½**

New York **7**

Nome **1**

Novosibirsk **19**

Osaka **21**

Palm Beach **7**

Paris **13**

Perth **20**

Reykjavik **12**

Rio de Janeiro **9**

Riyadh **15**

Rome **13**

San Francisco **4**

Santiago **8**

São Paulo **9**

Seoul **21**

Shanghai **20**

Singapore **20**

Stockholm **13**

Sverdlovsk **17**

Sydney **22**

Taipei **20**

Tel Aviv **14**

Tokyo **21**

Toronto **7**

Vancouver **4**

Vladivostok **21**

Washington, D.C. **7**

Wellington **24**

Winnipeg **6**

Yakutsk **21**

Zurich **13**

HOLIDAYS, TIME ZONES, AND CULTURAL TIPS BY COUNTRY

INTRODUCTION

On the following pages, 77 countries and their holidays are listed.

All of these countries have at least one day per week on which people do not work. Calendars were originally devised for religious purposes, so the day off work is usually the Sabbath. In countries with Christian majorities, Sunday is the usual day of rest. To align their work weeks with Western nations, some countries without Christian majorities also take Sundays off. These include China, India, Indonesia, Japan, South Korea, Sri Lanka and Taiwan.

In countries with Muslim majorities, the Muslim Sabbath, Friday, is usually the day of rest. (This includes Egypt, Kuwait, Pakistan, Saudi Arabia, and some parts of Malaysia.) In Israel, the Sabbath is on Saturday. However, under both the Muslim and Jewish calendars, the Sabbath runs from sundown to sundown (not midnight to midnight, as it does in the Gregorian, or Western, calendar).

In regard to Islamic holidays, the Islamic calendar is a lunar calendar, and the exact dates of events can be altered by astronomical observations. We have included the predicted dates for Islamic holidays in this book. However, depending upon these observations, the actual dates can vary by a day either way. Executives should remember that business hours may vary during the holy month of Ramadan. Since the Muslim year is shorter than the Western one, the Western year 1999 spans two Ramadan celebrations. One will be (approximately) from December 20, 1998 through January 18, 1999. The second will be (approximately) from December 9, 1999 through January 4, 2000.

In the United States of America, each of the fifty states determines its own official holidays. It is important to consult the individual state listings for complete information about a particular state's holidays. The US Congress designates holidays only for Washington, D.C. and for federal employees.

Time zone information on each country is shown below the list of holidays. For help in determining the time difference between two countries, see the section on Time Difference Tables. Be aware that daylight savings time may be in effect in the counties concerned.

Finally, there are a few brief cultural tips for each country under the time zone information. These tips will assist both businesspeople and travelers who interact with the citizens of these countries.

Argentina

Jan	1	Fr	New Year's Day	Jul	9	Fr	Independence Day
Apr	1	Th	Holy Thursday	Aug	16	Fr	General José de San Martin Day observed
	2	Fr	Good Friday		17	Tu	General José de San Martin Day
May	1	Sa	Workers Day	Oct	11	Mo	Columbus Day observed
	25	Th	May Revolution 1810		12	Tu	Columbus Day
Jun	14	Mo	Malvinas Islands Memorial	Dec	8	We	Immaculate Conception
	20	Su	Flag Day		25	Sa	Christmas Day
	21	Mo	Flag Day observed		31	Fr	Bank Holiday

Standard time: Zone 9

- Argentines pride themselves on being more somber and businesslike than their neighbors (especially the Brazilians). To call someone or something "not serious" is one of the most damning accusations an Argentine can make.

- A formal, sober manner (with a firm handshake and good eye contact) is called for in Argentina.

- Dress tends to be formal in Argentina. Businessmen are not respected unless they wear a suit.

- Many Argentine executives work extended hours, sometimes lasting until 10:00 PM, so business meetings as late as 8:00 PM are not at all unusual.

- Vegetarians may have a hard time in Argentina, where the diet is heavily slanted towards meat. Argentina is a major cattle producer, and beef is served with most meals.

Australia

Jan	1	Fr	New Year's Day	May	3	Mo	Labor Day (Qld, NT)
	26	Tu	Australia Day		17	Mo	Adelaide Cup Day (SA)
Feb	9	Tu	Regatta Day (Tas)	Jun	7	Mo	Foundation Day (WA)
Mar	1	Mo	Eight-Hour Day (Tas)		14	Mo	Queen's Birthday (ACT, NSW)
	1	Mo	Labor Day (WA)	Aug	2	Mo	Bank holiday (ACT, NSW, NT, VIC, Tas, SA, NT, Qld)
	1	Mo	Labor Day (Vic)	Sep	27	Mo	Queen's Birthday (WA)
	15	Mo	Canberra Day (ACT)	Oct	4	Mo	Labor Day (ACT, NSW, SA)
Apr	2	Fr	Good Friday	Dec	25	Sa	Christmas Day
	5	Mo	Easter Monday		26	Su	Boxing Day
	6	Tu	Easter Tuesday (Tas)		27	Mo	Christmas holiday
	25	Su	ANZAC Day		28	Tu	Christmas holiday (Tas, WA, NT)
	26	Mo	ANZAC Day holiday (ACT, NSW, SA, WA, NT, Qld)		28	Tu	Proclamation Day (SA)

Standard time: Zones 20, 21, 22, 23
    Western Australia: Zone 20
    Northern Territory: Zone 21½
    South Australia: Zone 21½
    New South Wales; Australian Capital Territory; Queensland; Victoria;
    Tasmania: Zone 22

- High pressure sales and hype tends to be unsuccessful in Australia.

- Modesty is considered a virtue. Avoid touting your own skills or education. People are judged on their performance, not their training.

- Australians tend to be casual and informal. They may address you on a first-name basis.

- Diminutives are common in Australian slang. *Australian* is reduced to *Aussie, Australian Rules Football* is altered to *footie, barbecue* is shortened to *barby* or *barbie,* and *mosquito* becomes *mozzie.*

- Many Australians find argument to be entertaining. Conciliatory people who fail to express an opinion are not widely respected.

- Australia is one of the most egalitarian nations on Earth. In many taxis, a solo passenger should expect to ride in the front; to sit alone in the back is seen as "putting on airs."

Austria

Jan	1	Fr	New Year's Day	Aug	15	Su	Assumption
	6	We	Epiphany	Oct	26	Tu	National Day
Apr	5	Mo	Easter Monday	Nov	1	Mo	All Saints Day
May	1	Sa	Labor Day	Dec	8	We	Immaculate Conception
	13	Th	Ascension Day		25	Sa	Christmas Day
	24	Mo	Whit Monday		26	Su	St. Stephen's Day
Jun	3	Th	Corpus Christi				

Standard time: Zone 13

- Once the seat of the huge Austro-Hungarian Empire, modern Austria has been drastically diminished in size and power. However, it is now much more ethnically homogeneous: today, most Austrians speak the Austrian dialect of German and are Roman Catholic.

- Change has not been good to Austria, and many Austrians are technologically conservative and suspicious of innovation.

- High-pressure tactics do not work well in Austria. Executives tend to be very charming, relaxed and unhurried.

- The Austrian management style emphasizes consensus-building and sophisticated "people skills." Confrontation is usually avoided, even if rules must be bent to do so.

- Austrians are proud of their cultural achievements. Austrian classical music is world renowned.

Azerbaijan

Jan	1	Fr	New Year's Day
	19	Tu	Eid Al Fitr[1]
	20	We	Day of the Martyrs
Mar	8	Mo	Women's Day
	20	Sa	Novruz Bayrami (2 days)
Apr	8	Th	Gurban Bayrami
May	28	Fr	Republic Day
Jun	15	Tu	National Salvation Day
Oct	9	Sa	Army and Navy Day
	18	Mo	National Independence Day
Nov	12	Fr	Constitution Day
	17	We	Day of National Revival
Dec	31	Fr	Solidarity Day

1. Date is approximate.

Standard time: Zone 16

- Azerbaijan was the Azerbaijan Soviet Socialist Republic until the breakup of the USSR in 1991. Many Azeris also live in northern Iran.

- In 1992 and 1993, Azerbaijan was engaged in a bloody conflict with neighboring Armenia. Armenians currently hold approximately 20% of former Azeri territory.

- Azeris see the USA as favoring Armenia (due to politically powerful Armenian-Americans). However, US-Azeri relationships have improved since 1997. To counter Iranian influence over its people, the Azeri government has even signed assistance agreements with Israel.

- Although Azerbaijan has a Muslim majority, it remains a secular state. It is currently following the model of secular Turkey, rather than theocratic Iran.

- In addition to its petroleum reserves, Azerbaijan has substantial mineral resources, ranging from iron to marble to clay.

- A popular Azeri game is *chavgan*, which is similar to field hockey but uses a rag ball.

Belgium

Jan	1	Fr	New Year's Day	May	24	Mo	Whit Monday
Apr	4	Su	Easter	Jul	21	We	Belgian National Day
	5	Mo	Easter Monday	Aug	15	Su	Assumption
May	1	Su	Labor Day	Nov	1	Mo	All Saints Day
	13	Th	Ascension		11	Th	Armistice Day
	23	Su	Pentecost	Dec	25	Sa	Christmas

Standard time: Zone 13

- Belgium has three linguistic groups. Most Belgians are native French or Flemish (a variant of Dutch) speakers, but there is a small German speaking population. Most Belgians speak at least two languages.
- Many Belgians feel that their country exemplifies the best of two worlds— the business acumen of the Dutch and the sophistication of the French.
- The majority (over 90%) of Belgians are Roman Catholics.
- Generally, Belgian executives are willing to listen and compromise.
- Executives who work with both the Dutch and the Belgians usually find the Belgians more open and flexible.

Belize

Jan	1	Fr	New Year's Day	Sep	10	Fr	St. George's Caye Day
Mar	9	Tu	Baron Bliss Day		21	Tu	Independence Day
Apr	2	Fr	Good Friday	Oct	12	Tu	Columbus Day
	3	Sa	Holy Saturday	Nov	19	Fr	Garifuna Settlement Day
	5	Mo	Easter Monday	Dec	25	Sa	Christmas Day
May	1	Sa	Labor Day		26	Su	Boxing Day
	24	Mo	Commonwealth Day				

Standard time: Zone 6

- Belize is Central America's youngest independent nation; it was the colony of British Honduras until 1981.

- Relations between Belize and its neighbors are now cordial, although Guatemala claimed parts of Belizean territory until 1992.

- Although Belize's official language is English, visitors should be warned that the Creole dialect of English spoken by most Belizeans is unintelligible to many foreign speakers of English. However, Belizean businesspeople can generally converse in conventional English.

- Business in Belize is concentrated in the areas of tourism, agriculture and forestry. However, Belize has recently become a banking haven.

- Citizenship in Belize is available for about US$50,000. Citizenship can be acquired without even visiting the country!

Bolivia

Jan	1	Fr	New Year's Day	Jun	3	Th	Corpus Christi
Feb	15	Mo	Carnival Monday	Aug	6	Fr	Independence Day
	16	Tu	Carnival	Nov	1	Mo	All Saints Day
Apr	2	Fr	Good Friday	Dec	25	Sa	Christmas Day
May	1	Sa	Labor Day				

Standard time: Zone 8

- Bolivians appreciate visitors knowing something about their history. Long before European settlements were founded in the USA, the Bolivian silver-mining center of Potosí was the largest Spanish colonial city in the Western hemisphere.

- Chile seized Bolivia's only outlet to the sea in 1883, and the loss of their seacoast is still a sore spot to Bolivians.

- Most Bolivians are of mixed Spanish and Indian heritage, and many speak an Amerindian language. Executives speak Spanish.

- The Spanish dialect spoken in Bolivia is very conservative. Unlike the Spanish used in most of Latin America, Bolivians retain the second-person plural (*vosotros*) form of verbs.

- Business is conducted at a leisurely pace in Bolivia. Social relationships must be established before business commences.

- Foreign visitors to Bolivia are at risk of altitude sickness. Altitude sickness presents a problem in areas over 6,000 feet above sea level. There is no effective predictor of who will succumb and who won't. People of different ages, sexes, and health may be affected.

- The best way to avoid altitude sickness is to acclimate yourself. Once you get to 6,000 feet, you should ideally spend at least two nights at that altitude, repeating this acclimation period at each increase of 3,000 feet. La Paz, the capital, is at 13,000 feet.

Brazil

Jan	1	Fr	New Year's Day		Jun	3	Th	Corpus Christi
Feb	15	Mo	Carnival Monday		Oct	12	Tu	Our Lady Aparecida
	16	Tu	Carnival		Nov	1	Mo	All Saints Day
	17	We	Ash Wednesday			2	Tu	All Souls Day
Apr	1	Th	Holy Thursday			15	Mo	Proclamation of the Republic
	2	Fr	Good Friday		Dec	8	We	Immaculate Conception
	3	Sa	Holy Saturday			24	Fr	Christmas Eve
	21	We	Tiradentes Day			25	Sa	Christmas Day
May	1	Sa	Labor Day			31	Fr	New Year's Eve

Standard time: Zone 7, 8, 9
    Western Brazil: Zone 7
    Central Brazil: Zone 8
    Coastal states, capital: Zone 9

- Brazil is Latin America's largest and most populous country. It is difficult to make generalizations about such a huge and diverse nation. Many Brazilians can trace their ancestry to Portugal, Africa, Germany and Asia—as well as to the indigenous (Amerindian) peoples.

- A former colony of Portugal, Brazil's official language is Portuguese. But some 200 different languages are spoken throughout Brazil! Many executives have some familiarity with English.

- Visitors usually comment on the charm and friendliness of Brazilians. Social skills are necessary for business success in Brazil.

- Brazilians are proud of their cultural achievements in the arts. Many Brazilian writers and musicians are known throughout the world, and visitors should have some familiarity with them.

- Most of Latin America watches US television shows dubbed into Spanish. Brazilian networks are also full of Brazilian-produced TV shows, including immensely-popular soap operas (*telenovas*).

Canada

Jan	1	Fr	New Year's Day	Jul	1	Th	Canada Day
	4	Mo	New Year's holiday (Quebec)	Aug	2	Mo	Civic holiday
Feb	15	Mo	Family Day (Alberta)		20	Fr	Discovery Day (Yukon)
	19	Fr	Heritage Day	Sep	6	Mo	Labor Day
Apr	2	Fr	Good Friday	Oct	11	Mo	Thanksgiving
	5	Mo	Easter Monday	Nov	11	Th	Remembrance Day
May	24	Mo	Victoria Day	Dec	27	Mo	Christmas Day observed
Jun	24	Th	St. Jean Baptiste Day (Quebec)		28	Tu	Boxing Day

Standard time: Zone 4, 5, 6, 7, 8, 8½

    Pacific (Whitehorse, Vancouver): Zone 4

    Mountain (Calgary, Yellowknife, Edmonton): Zone 5

    Central (Regina): Zone 6

    Central (Winnipeg): Zone 7

    Eastern (Ottawa, Toronto, Montreal): Zone 7

    Atlantic (Saint John, Halifax): Zone 8

    Newfoundland (Saint John's): Zone 8½

- Québecois separatism remains an issue. Canada is unique among industrialized countries in that its future as a unified nation remains in doubt.

- Canadians are very protective of their "Canadian identity," and are quick to point out people and innovations from Canada.

- Although foreigners may have difficulty differentiating between citizens of Canada and the USA, that difference is important to Canadians.

- Aggressive sales tactics which are successful in the USA may fail when used on the more reserved Canadians.

- Canada is a multicultural nation. Although the majority are French or English/Irish/Scots, there are many Canadians of Amerindian, German and Ukrainian descent. Many of the newest Canadians were born in Asia, especially in British Columbia. Each ethnic group has its own customs.

- Many Canadian Amerindians prefer the term "First Nation" to "Native American." They generally consider themselves culturally distinct from the Inuit (Eskimo) people.

Chile

Jan	1	Fr	New Year's Day	Sep	18	Sa	Independence Day
Apr	2	Fr	Good Friday		19	Su	Armed Forces Day
	3	Sa	Holy Saturday	Oct	12	Tu	Columbus Day
May	1	Sa	Labor Day	Nov	1	Mo	All Saints Day
	21	Fr	Battle of Iquique	Dec	8	We	Immaculate Conception
Jun	29	Tu	Sts. Peter and Paul		25	Sa	Christmas Day
Aug	15	Su	Assumption				

Standard time: Zone 8

- Chile's unique geography has shaped its society in many ways. The population is ethnically homogeneous (about 90% mestizo). Linguistically isolated, Chileans speak a conservative form of Spanish.

- Although only a small number of Chileans regularly attend Mass, the Catholic Church remains politically powerful. Divorce remains illegal due to the Church's influence.

- Several countries have attempted to copy the economic success of General Augusto Pinochet's eight-year rule, although none have been successful in duplicating the "Chilean Model."

- The 1998 arrest of General Pinochet in the UK has brought the human-rights abuses of his dictatorship to the attention of the world. But some of the same Chileans who suffered under his leadership protested his arrest, considering it a violation of Chile's sovereignty.

- Chileans are disappointed by their failure to be quickly admitted to the North American Free Trade Agreement (NAFTA). In addition, Chile's substantial trade with Asia has diminished due to the 1998 Asian economic meltdown.

China

Jan	1	Fr	New Year's Day	Jun	18	Fr	Dragon Boat Festival
Feb	16	Tu	Spring Festival (2 days)	Jul	1	Th	Founding of the Communist Party
Mar	2	Tu	Lantern Festival	Aug	1	Su	Birthday of the People's Liberation Army
	8	Mo	Women's Day	Sep	24	Fr	Mid-Autumn Festival
May	1	Sa	Labor Day	Oct	1	Fr	National Day
	4	Tu	Youth Day		2	Sa	National Day
Jun	1	Tu	Children's Day				

Standard time: Zone 20

- China is a hierarchical society. Confucianism gives a ranking to every individual, and deference to those of higher rank is expected. Business-people acquire status through age, wealth, occupation and influence. When a delegation enters a room, the party is arranged by rank, with the highest-ranking person entering first, followed by the second-highest, and so on. On the other hand, at a banquet, the most important person is the last to arrive and the first to leave.

- Most Chinese follow various folk beliefs which designate auspicious and unlucky things. For example, the number four is considered unlucky, and many Chinese buildings do not have a fourth floor (in skyscrapers, the number is simply skipped, just as some Western buildings have no thirteenth floor). The color red is considered auspicious, so it is used for many things—but not to write personal names, since names are tradi-tionally written in red after a person has died. Many business deals are only signed on an astrologically auspicious day and hour.

- Business cards are important in China. Your card should be written in your native language on one side, and in Chinese on the back. Present your card with the Chinese-side up. Gold lettering is the most presti-gious color for business cards. Be sure that the Chinese translation is done by someone familiar with the linguistic revisions made in Communist China. (Taiwan still uses traditional Chinese, and a card or promotional material translated into old-style Chinese will not be well received in the People's Republic of China.)

- Most ethnic Chinese have three names. The surname is given first, followed by the two given names. For example, in the name Chang Wu Jiang, Chang is his surname, and he would be called Mr. Chang. In English, the two given names are often written as one name in the PRC, so Chang Wu Jiang could be written as Chang Wujiang. In the past, Hong Kong Chinese usually hyphenated their given names (Chang Wu-jiang). Chinese executives who deal often with foreigners may adopt a Western given name.

- Married women in China do not traditionally take their husband's surname. It is correct to address a married woman as Madam, followed by her surname.

Colombia

Jan	1	Fr	New Year's Day	Jun	14	Mo	Sacred Heart of Jesus
	11	Mo	Epiphany	Jul	5	Mo	Sts. Peter and Paul
Feb	17	We	Ash Wednesday		20	Tu	Independence Day
Mar	22	Mo	St. Joseph's Day	Aug	7	Sa	Battle of Boyacá
Apr	1	Th	Holy Thursday		16	Mo	Assumption
	2	Fr	Good Friday	Oct	18	Mo	Columbus Day
	3	Su	Easter	Nov	1	Mo	All Saints Day
May	1	Sa	Labor Day		15	Mo	Independence of Cartegena
	17	Mo	Ascension	Dec	8	We	Immaculate Conception
Jun	7	Mo	Corpus Christi		25	Sa	Christmas Day

Standard time: Zone 7

- Colombia's rugged geography has kept its multiracial population in isolated groups. The descendants of the Spanish settlers are concentrated in the Antioquia department (which includes Medellín), plus the coffee-growing regions. Colombia's African population is concentrated in coastal areas, especially the Chocó department and the nearby city of Cali. The Amerindians are widely scattered, many living in the jungle areas along tributaries of the Amazon River.

- The official language of Colombia is Spanish (which Colombians call *castellano*, not *español*). Colombians have many regional terms, which are collectively known as colombianismos. English is not widely spoken, so expect to use interpreters and have all materials translated into Spanish.

- Colombia has a reputation (which may or may not be deserved) as the most dangerous nation for foreigners to visit in Latin America. The danger to foreigners comes not from narcoterrorists but kidnappers, who hold businesspeople for ransom.

- Long before it became known for narcotrafficing, Colombia had a reputation as a haven for smugglers. Colombian emeralds and exotic birds were smuggled out, and consumer goods were smuggled in to evade high taxes.

- Colombians are known for their extended greetings. Every conversation seems to begin with in-depth inquiries as to the health, welfare, location and status of the speakers and their relatives. Visitors who attempt to shorten this greeting are considered impolite.

Costa Rica

Jan	1	Fr	New Year's Day	Aug	2	Mo	Our Lady of the Angels
Mar	19	Fr	St. Joseph's Day		15	Su	Assumption/Mother's Day
Apr	1	Th	Holy Thursday	Sep	15	We	Independence Day
	2	Fr	Good Friday	Oct	12	Tu	Columbus Day
	11	Su	National Heroes Day	Dec	25	Sa	Christmas Day
May	1	Sa	Labor Day		29	We	National holiday
Jun	29	Tu	Sts. Peter and Paul		30	Th	National holiday
Jul	25	Su	Annexation of Guana-caste		31	Fr	National holiday

Standard time: Zone 6

- Although the official language is Spanish, the large number of North Americans in Costa Rica has made English a virtual second language.

- Even though almost all Costa Rican executives speak English, all written materials should be translated into Spanish.

- The Costa Rican government is supportive of foreign business. *Exportar es Bueno* (*Export is Good*) is an official slogan.

- While it is often pointed out that peaceful Costa Rica has no Army, it has plenty of other law enforcement personnel. These range from the police, to the Civil Guard, to the commandos of the Immediate Action Unit. In addition, the official US presence (largely through USAID, the US Agency for International Development) is so pervasive that some consider it a "parallel government."

- Costa Ricans call themselves *ticos* (the feminine form is *ticas*).

Cuba

Jan	1	Fr	National Liberation Day	Jul	25	Su	National Rebellion Day (3 days)
Feb	24	We	Baire Proclamation	Oct	10	Su	Beginning of the Wars of Independence
Apr	19	Mo	Victory at Giron	Dec	25	Sa	Christmas Day
May	1	Sa	International Labor Day				

Standard time: Zone 7

- The United States of America maintains heavy restrictions on contact with Cuba. The 1996 Helms-Burton Act allows fines of up to $50,000 to be imposed on US citizens who visit Cuba without US permission. The US government grants this permission for a number of reasons (including journalists and persons with relatives in Cuba). However, at this writing, permission is not granted for the purposes of business or tourism.

- Cuba welcomes US citizens whether or not they are traveling with permission of their government. Since US visitors with a Cuban stamp in their passports may be penalized upon their return to the US, most Cuban immigration officers will, upon request, stamp a separate document (such as a visa) instead of a passport.

- Although Cubans blame US policy for their economic problems, there is little animosity against individual visitors from the USA.

- Since US-Cuba trade is virtually nonexistent, Cuba's largest trade partner is now Canada. Trade between Russia and Cuba still exists, but is drastically reduced from previous levels.

- The US dollar (known locally as the *divisa*) is the unofficial currency of Cuba. Even in establishments where Cubans pay in non-convertible Cuban pesos (*moneda nacional*), foreigners are often expected to pay with hard currency—either dollars or convertible Cuban pesos (*peso convertible*).

Czech Republic

Jan	1	Fr	New Year's Day	Jul	6	Tu	Jan Hus Day
Apr	5	Mo	Easter Monday	Oct	28	Th	Independence Day
May	1	Sa	Labor Day	Dec	24	Fr	Christmas Eve
	8	Sa	Liberation Day		25	Sa	Christmas Day
Jul	5	Mo	Sts. Cyril and Method-ius		26	Su	Christmas holiday

Standard time: Zone 13

- Prague has become a magnet for young Western expatriates. Czechs have become used to dealing with English-speakers.

- During the Communist era (1945-1989), industrial pollution was seen as a sign of industrial progress. Since then, pollution control and environmental stewardship have become important to Czechs.

- In 1993, the former Czechoslovakia split into two nations: the Czech Republic and Slovakia. The Czech Republic is the most economically successful of the former Warsaw Pact nations.

- While most Czechs look forward to eventually becoming members of the European Union, they tend to be less approving of Czech membership in NATO. This is especially true of the expense they must incur to bring their military up to NATO standards.

Denmark

Jan	1	Fr	New Year's Day	May	13	Th	Ascension
Apr	1	Th	Holy Thursday		23	Su	Whitsunday
	2	Fr	Good Friday		24	Mo	Whit Monday
	4	Su	Easter Sunday	Jun	5	Sa	Constitution Day
	5	Mo	Easter Monday	Dec	24	Fr	Christmas Eve
	30	Fr	General Prayer Day		25	Sa	Christmas Day
May	1	Sa	Workers' Day		26	Su	Christmas holiday

Standard time: Zone 13

- Denmark was ranked first out of 85 nations in Transparency International's 1998 Corruption Perceptions Index. Curiously, despite Denmark's rating as the most corruption-free country in the world, Danes do not tend to regard rules as inflexible. Finding ways to get around regulations is regarded as a sport by many.

- Danes tend to maintain a strict divide between their business and family lives. Most do not like working overtime, and are unwilling to discuss business matters except during office hours.

- High income taxes discourage making money in Denmark, so many Danish entrepreneurs seek their fortunes abroad.

- The Danes held overseas possessions into modern times. Denmark sold its Virgin Islands to the USA in 1917, and Iceland declared itself independent in 1944. Today, only Greenland and the Faroe Islands remain under Danish rule.

- Danish executives have a reputation among other Scandinavians as sharp businesspeople.

Dominican Republic

Jan	1	Fr	New Year's Day	May	1	Sa	Labor Day
	6	We	Feast of Three Kings	Jun	3	Th	Corpus Christi
	21	Th	Our Lady of Altagracia	Aug	16	Mo	Restoration of the Republic
	26	Tu	Duarte's Day	Sep	24	Fr	Our Lady of Las Mercedes
Feb	27	Sa	Independence Day	Oct	12	Tu	Columbus Day
Apr	2	Fr	Good Friday	Dec	25	Sa	Christmas Day

Standard time: Zone 8

- The Dominican Republic was the oldest of Spain's New World colonies. Christopher Columbus claimed it for Spain on his first voyage in 1492.

- The Dominican Republic occupies about two-thirds of the island of Hispanola. The rest of the island makes up the Republic of Haiti. While the Dominican Republic is not a wealthy nation, immigrants from poverty-stricken Haiti often cross the border, creating tensions between the two countries.

- While the heritage of the Dominican Republic is Spanish, its most important influence is the USA. The USA has intervened in Dominican affairs many times. The USA is its largest trading partner, and many Dominicans have relatives in the USA.

Ecuador

Jan	1	Fr	New Year's Day	Oct	9	Sa	Guayaquil Independence Day
Apr	2	Fr	Good Friday	Nov	2	Tu	All Souls Day
May	1	Sa	Labor Day		3	We	Cuenca Independence Day
Aug	10	Tu	Independence Day	Dec	25	Sa	Christmas Day

Standard time: Zone 7

- The name *Ecuador* is derived from the word *equator*. Like most equatorial locales, Ecuador tends to be hot (except in the highlands). Despite a climate that is often uncomfortably hot and humid, businessmen are expected to wear a suit and tie.

- Formality tends to increase as you go inland. Customs and dress on the coast are more casual than in the Ecuadorian interior.

- Ecuador has suffered numerous natural disasters, such as a major earthquake in 1987 and periodic climactic disruptions attributed to El Niño.

- Fighting broke out in 1995 between Ecuador and Peru over the disputed border in the Cordillera del Cóndor region. Since then, the dispute has been referred to international arbitration. Relations between Ecuador and Peru have improved but remain tense.

- Until oil exportation began in 1972, Ecuador was the quintessential "banana republic" —small, poor and agricultural.

- Although oil exportation has brought billions of dollars into Ecuador's economy, this is (at best) a mixed blessing. Relatively few Ecuadorians have profited from the oil boom, while most citizens have suffered from rampant inflation and environmental degradation. In any Ecuadorian city, you can see the graffito *Más petróleo = más pobreza* (*More petroleum = more poverty*).

Egypt

Jan	7	Th	Christmas (Coptic Christians)	May	1	Sa	Labor Day
	18	Mo	Ramadan Bairam (3 days)	Jun	23	We	Revolution Anniversary
Mar	27	Sa	Wakfet Arafet		26	Sa	Mawled El-Nabi
	28	Su	Courban Bairam (4 days)	Oct	6	We	Armed Forces Day
Apr	11	Su	Easter Sunday		23	Sa	National Liberation Day
	12	Mo	Sham El Nessim (2 days)		24	Su	Suez Victory Day
	17	Sa	New Year's Day	Dec	23	Th	Victory Day
	25	Su	Sinai Liberation Day				

Standard time: Zone 14

- Egypt is one of the most Westernized nations of the Middle East. You will encounter some international executives who are very familiar with Western business customs. Other Egyptian executives may have traditional Arab manners. Be prepared for any variation.

- While Egyptians often gesture with their hands while speaking, they do not point at another person. Pointing at people is very impolite.

- As a general rule, keep both feet on the ground. Traditional Arabs do not cross their legs when sitting. Never show the bottom of your foot to an Arab; this is considered offensive. Even when one removes one's shoes (as when entering a Mosque), the soles of the shoes are placed together, preventing the sole from being pointed at anyone.

- The "thumbs up" gesture is offensive throughout the Arab world.

- An Egyptian gesture meaning "calm down" or "wait a minute" is accomplished in this way: with your palm facing you, touch all your fingers to your thumb, then bob your hand up and down (as if you were weighing something).

- Adjustments foreigners must make include the workweek (Friday is the Islamic Sabbath, so the workweek runs Saturday through Wednesday) and Ramadan (the month of fasting, when no one eats or drinks during the day).

- Saving face is always a consideration in Egypt. Never cause someone to be embarrassed in public. Be prepared to go to great lengths to protect someone's dignity.

El Salvador

Jan	1	Fr	New Year's Day	Aug	6	Fr	San Salvador Feast
Mar	31	We	Holy Wednesday	Sep	15	We	Independence Day
Apr	1	Th	Holy Thursday	Nov	2	Tu	All Souls Day
	2	Fr	Good Friday	Dec	24	Fr	Christmas Eve
May	1	Sa	Labor Day		25	Sa	Christmas Day
Aug	4	We	San Salvador Feast		31	Fr	Bank holiday
	5	Th	San Salvador Feast				

Standard time: Zone 6

- The only Central American nation without a coastline on the Caribbean, El Salvador is also the smallest and most densely populated country in Central America. Salvadorans have frequently left to seek work in neighboring countries, which is a cause for friction with Salvador's neighbors.

- In 1980, two events brought El Salvador worldwide notoriety: the assassination of Catholic Archbishop Oscar Arnulfo Romero (a nominee for the Nobel Peace Prize), and the rape and murder of four Maryknoll nuns from the USA. Both actions were traced to Salvadoran death-squads.

- The 1992 peace accords ended more than a decade of civil war between the government and guerrillas. An estimated 70,000 Salvadorans lost their lives, and more than 750,000 fled the country.

- Salvadorans have learned the dangers of depending upon a single crop. In the 1920s, 95% of El Salvador's export earnings came from coffee. But the demand for coffee plummeted during the Great Depression, impoverishing thousands of Salvadorans. Although the banana harvest was badly damaged by Hurricane Mitch in 1998, bananas rank behind sugarcane and coffee as Salvador's largest crops.

- El Salvador has been an oligarchy ever since independence. The original *Fourteen Families* (*Los Catorce*) who ran the country for their benefit has expanded into about 250 families, but they continue to dominate the Salvadoran economy.

Fiji

Jan	1	Fr	New Year's Day	Jun	28	Mo	Prophet Mohammed's Birthday
Mar	12	Fr	National Youth Day	Jul	26	Mo	Constitution Day
Apr	2	Fr	Good Friday	Oct	11	Mo	Fiji Day
	3	Sa	Easter Saturday	Nov	8	Mo	Diwali
	5	Mo	Easter Monday	Dec	25	Sa	Christmas Day
May	31	Mo	Ratu Sir Lala Sukuna Day		27	Mo	Boxing Day
Jun	12	Sa	Queen's Birthday				

Standard time: Zone 24

- Fiji's population is almost evenly split between ethnic Fijians (51%) and Indians (43%). The two groups have very different customs and traditions.

- Friction between Fijians and Indians, which led to coups in 1987, has diminished but not disappeared. The new constitution (effective July 1998) guarantees a multiracial Cabinet.

- Fiji is still recovering from the effects of Cyclone Gavin, which struck in March 1997.

- Christian missionaries from the US and UK have had a strong influence on the ethnic Fijians.

- Most ethnic Fijians live in small villages; the Indians are concentrated in the towns. Most of Fiji's businesses are owned and run by Indians.

Finland

Jan	1	Fr	New Year's Day	May	23	Su	Whitsun
	6	We	Epiphany	Jun	25	Fr	Midsummer (2 days)
Apr	2	Fr	Good Friday	Nov	6	Sa	All Saints Day
	4	Su	Easter	Dec	6	Mo	Independence Day
	5	Mo	Easter Monday		24	Fr	Christmas Eve
	30	Fr	May Day Eve		25	Sa	Christmas Day
May	1	Sa	May Day		26	Su	Boxing Day
	13	Th	Ascension				

Standard time: Zone 14

- Both Finnish and Swedish are official languages. Unlike most European tongues, Finnish is not an Indo-European language. Finnish is in the Finno-Ugric linguistic group, along with Estonian and Hungarian.

- Although Norwegian, Swedish and Danish are all mutually intelligible, Finnish is not.

- The Finns are considered to be the quietest people in Europe. Long and frequent silences are typical. Executives who become nervous during long pauses will lose when negotiating with Finns.

- After decades of threats from the USSR, Finland now profits from its proximity to Russia. Some manufacturers have built factories in Finland near the border, building goods for export into Russia. Rather than build factories in Russia, they take advantage of Finland's stable laws and tax structure, as well as skilled Finnish labor.

- Punctuality is very important to the Finns. Along with the Germans and the Swiss, they are considered the most punctual people in Europe. Being late to an appointment is considered very bad form, although the reserved Finns will rarely remonstrate anyone for it.

France

- Conversation is considered an art to the French. French conversations are typically nonlinear. Cleverness is considered more important than accuracy or truth. Everyone speaks at once, interrupting each other, and finishing each other's sentences. Many foreigners consider this rude. (Most French find linear-thinking foreigners boring. To the French, such people don't converse, they lecture.)

- Apologies are heard much more frequently in the USA or the UK than in France. A French executive who admits error and apologizes has lost face. On the other hand, there is no shame in France to telling small lies or even (occasionally) cheating. Sometimes people accept a statement they know is untrue, rather than challenging it and causing the liar to lose dignity.

- US citizens, used to smiles everywhere, find the French somewhat staid. The French don't generally smile in public, or without a specific reason. To the French, a person smiling without cause is either an idiot or condescending.

- French attitudes towards time are different from those in the USA, the UK, or Germany. Surprisingly, a French businessperson might give an excuse for being a few minutes late to a meeting, yet say nothing if they're a half-hour late. No insult is intended by tardiness. To the French, life is complex, and many things happen which can cause delay. People and relationships are always more important than a soulless schedule. (There are a few exceptions—some executives now insist on punctuality from employees.)

- The French are second to none in appreciation of fine food. Eating remains one of life's greatest pleasures in France. But this is no excuse for gaining weight, and the French have a horror of becoming fat. (One of their favorite epithet for US citizens is "overfed Americans.")

- Clothes are very important in France. This is not surprising; the very words we use to describe fashion—*chic, panache, haute couture*—are from the French language. Not everyone in France owns an extensive wardrobe, but what they do own is expensive, well made, and fashionable. Affluent executives wear suits every single day. They also tend to have great posture, which makes their clothes look even better.

Germany

Jan	1	Fr	New Year's Eve	Jun	3	Th	Corpus Christi
	6	We	Epiphany[1]	Aug	15	Su	Assumption[2]
Apr	2	Fr	Good Friday	Oct	3	Su	Day of German Unity
	4	Su	Easter		31	Su	Reformation Day
	5	Mo	Easter Monday	Nov	1	Mo	All Saints Day
May	1	Sa	May Day		17	We	Repentence Day[3]
	13	Th	Ascension	Dec	25	Sa	Christmas Day
	23	Su	Pentecost		26	Su	Second Day of Christmas
	24	Mo	Pentecost Monday				

1. Baden-Wuerttemberg, Bavaria Saxony-Anhalt
2. Bavaria, Saarland
3. Saxony

Standard time: Zone 13

- As befits Europe's most populous nation, there is a lot of diversity in Germany. Many of the stereotypes of Germans do not hold true in every region, and some are not true at all. In addition, there are many residents who came from other nations to work in Germany, especially from Turkey. In the past, they and their children could never become German citizens, but these restrictions on citizenship are being changed.

- The Germans have a reputation for hard work. While this is generally true, the German worker is not *at* work often. German workers get more time off than almost any other laborers in the world. The law mandates a full 30 days of paid vacation—not to mention paid holidays and generous sick leave. To the dismay of German business leaders, it costs more to hire a German laborer than a worker in any other country on the planet.

- A reverence for nature (especially the primeval forest) is often given as a German characteristic. As evidence of this, Germany has passed strict pollution and recycling laws. However, these laws were only established after terrible damage was done to German rivers and forests.

- Germany and France have frequently been rivals. Curiously, both countries revere Charlemagne as their founder, since his empire spanned much of modern-day France and Germany. The Germans refer to him as *Karl der Grosse* (*Karl the Great*). As a cultural icon for both peoples, Charlemagne is equally popular in both nations.

- The 1990 reunification of East and West Germany has brought economic hardship. It will be years before the former East Germans can match West Germany's standard of living.

Greece

Jan	1	Fr	New Year's Eve	May	1	Sa	Labor Day
	6	We	Epiphany		31	Mo	Whit Monday
Feb	22	Mo	Monday in Lent	Aug	15	Su	Assumption
Mar	25	Th	Independence Day	Oct	28	Th	Ochi Day
Apr	9	Fr	Good Friday	Dec	25	Sa	Christmas Day
	12	Mo	Easter Monday		26	Su	Boxing Day

Standard time: Zone 14

- Compared to other members of the European Union, Greece has the largest percentage of people working in agriculture. Around 20% of Greeks work in agriculture, compared to less than 6% in most industrialized countries.

- The Greek Orthodox Church forms an integral part of the Greek identity. Unlike Western branches of Christianity, Greek Orthodoxy stresses individual choice and does not emphasize guilt or shame. Some view this as a defining aspect of the Greek character.

- Today, the Greek people speak a form of the Greek language known as Demotic Greek. This is a modern form of the Ancient Greek spoken two thousand years ago. Classical Studies programs usually teach Ancient Greek, not modern Demotic Greek.

- The Greek people tend to be physically demonstrative. They kiss, hug, and walk arm-in-arm with both relatives and friends. Even Greek soldiers often walk arm-in-arm. This is not private behavior; it can be seen every day in the streets, to a degree that surprises visitors from Northern Europe and North America.

- Greek (also called Hellenic) is written in the Greek alphabet, rather than the Roman alphabet used by most Western European nations. (Even Turkey uses the Roman alphabet.) The Cyrillic alphabet used by the Russians and Bulgarians is derived from this Greek alphabet.

- Although Greece and Turkey are both members of NATO, the two countries have a long history of animosity, and have been on the verge of full-scale war several times since 1945. The most serious event occurred in 1974 over the island of Cyprus, when Greek and Turkish troops battled each other. Thanks to UN intervention and peacekeeping troops, Cyprus is now divided between Greek areas and Turkish areas.

Guatemala

Jan	1	Fr	New Year's Day	Sep	15	We	Independence Day
Mar	31	We	Holy Wednesday	Oct	12	Tu	Day of the Race
Apr	1	Th	Holy Thursday		20	We	Revolution Day
	2	Fr	Good Friday	Nov	1	Mo	All Saints Day
	3	Sa	Holy Saturday	Dec	24	Fr	Christmas Eve
May	1	Sa	Labor Day		25	Sa	Christmas Day
Jun	30	We	Army Day		31	Fr	New Year's Eve
Aug	15	Su	Assumption				

Standard time: Zone 6

- The inhabitants of Guatemala refer to themselves as *guatemaltecos*. Although exact population figures are in dispute, Guatemala's citizens are about equally divided between Amerindians and mestizos (persons of mixed Amerindian and Hispanic ancestry). Guatemala has the largest Amerindian population in Central America.

- Although not as hard-hit as its neighbor by Hurricane Mitch in 1998, Guatemala nevertheless sustained serious damage.

- Until recently, Guatemalans had suffered *thirty-six years* of civil war—the longest-running insurgency in Latin America. A peace treaty was implemented in 1996, signed by President Alvaro Arzu, Rolando Moran (leader of the URNG guerrilla front) and Amerindian peace activist Rigoberta Menchú (1992 winner of the Nobel Peace Prize). The treaty calls for land, judicial and other reforms.

- International observers have praised the efforts of President Arzu to put the peace treaty reforms into effect. In 1998, however, Bishop Juan Gerardi was murdered two days after submitting a report on government human-rights abuses. This has put the effectiveness of reforms in doubt.

- The conditions of the Peace Accords include the reduction of the Army and the creation of a new Guatemalan police force. The police are being trained by Spain's *Guardia Civil*. Guatemalan forces have often been trained by foreigners, including advisors from the USA, Argentina, Taiwan and Israel.

Honduras

Jan	1	Fr	New Year's Day	Sep	15	We	Independence Day
Apr	1	Th	Holy Thursday	Oct	3	Su	Francisco Morazan's Birthday
	2	Fr	Good Friday		12	Tu	Columbus Day
	14	We	Pan American Day		21	Th	Armed Forces Day
May	1	Sa	Labor Day	Dec	25	Sa	Christmas Day

Standard time: Zone 6

- The Hondurans refer to themselves as *Hondureños*. Unlike its neighbors, Honduras was not historically dominated by a landholding elite. After independence from Spain, northern Honduras was controlled by foreign-owned banana companies. These companies were often more influential than the government at Tegucigalpa.

- During colonial times, Honduras was the wealthiest country in Central America: the Spanish discovered gold and silver near Tegucigalpa in the 1570s. But once the precious metals ran out, Honduras became a poor agricultural nation, dependent upon its banana crop. Only recently, with diversification, has the middle class of Honduras grown.

- Hurricane Mitch devastated Honduras in late 1998. Damage to its infrastructure and agriculture (primarily coffee and banana crops) has been estimated at US$4 billion—roughly equivalent to its annual GNP.

- Honduras fought a short war with neighboring El Salvador in 1969. It became known as the *Soccer War*, since the precipitating incident was an attack on Honduran soccer fans at a World Cup qualifying game in San Salvador. However, the actual cause was the influx of Salvadoran immigrants living and working in Honduras. Tiny El Salvador is overpopulated, while large Honduras has a much lower population density. But both countries are very poor, and Hondurans saw illegal Salvadoran immigrants as taking work and vital resources from Hondurans.

- Honduras' capital and largest city is Tegucigalpa (colloquially known as *Tegus*, pronounced *"TEY-goose"*). Many Honduran corporations have their offices in Tegucigalpa. However, Honduras' boom town is its second-largest city, San Pedro Sula. Before Hurricane Mitch, San Pedro Sula was the fastest-growing city in Central America.

Hungary

Jan	1	Fr	New Year's Day	Aug	20	Fr	Constitution Day
Mar	15	Mo	Anniversary of Hungarian Revolution	Oct	23	Sa	Republic Day
Apr	5	Mo	Easter Monday	Dec	25	Sa	Christmas Day
May	1	Sa	Labor Day		26	Su	Christmas holiday
	24	Mo	Whit Monday				

Standard time: Zone 13

- The Hungarian language is called Magyar, and it is difficult for English-speakers to learn. Unlike most European languages, Magyar is not a member of the Indo-European linguistic family. Magyar is a Finno-Ugric tongue, distantly related to Finnish and Estonian. Fortunately, Hungarians have a tradition of learning other languages, and it is not difficult to find Hungarians to translate into English.

- In Hungary, the surname is traditionally given before the given name. The Hungarian musicians we know as Béla Bartók and Zoltán Kodály are known in their homeland as Bartók Béla and Kodály Zoltán. The Hungarian equivalents of Mr. (*ur*), Mrs. (*ne* or *asszony*) and Miss (*kisasszony*) follow the last name; *Mr. Bartók* would be *Bartók ur.*

Iceland

Jan	1	Fr	New Year's Day	May	24	Mo	Whit Monday
Apr	1	Th	Holy Thursday	Jun	17	Th	National Day
	2	Fr	Good Friday	Aug	2	Mo	Bank holiday
	5	Mo	Easter Monday	Dec	24	Fr	Christmas Eve
	22	Th	First Day of Summer		25	Sa	Christmas Day
May	1	Sa	Labor Day		26	Su	Boxing Day
	13	Th	Ascension Day		31	Fr	New Year's Eve

Standard time: Zone 12

- The national language is Icelandic, although both English and Danish are widely spoken. The Icelandic alphabet has two letters which no longer appear in English (although they can be found in Old English texts).

- Virtually all Icelandic surnames are patronymics: they are derived from the first name of each individual's father. The surnames of Icelandic women end in -*dottir* ("daughter") while male surnames end in -*son*. (For example, *Thordis Eríksdóttir* means *Thordis, daughter of Erik*; Thordis' brother *Davíd* would be *Davíd Erikson*.) Notice that Icelandic men and women do not share the same surnames, even if they are married or related.

- Icelanders are addressed by their full name or title and first name, but never by their surname alone. (For example, the President of Iceland is *Ólafur Ragnar Grímsson*. He could be addressed by his full name, or as *President Ólafur*, but never as *President Grímsson*.)

- Most Icelanders belong to the Evangelical Lutheran Church, also called the Church of Iceland.

- Thanks primarily to the export of fish, Icelanders today enjoy a high standard of living, comparable to that of the USA. As Iceland's primary natural resource, the country is adamant about preserving its fisheries. This frequently puts it into conflict with other fishing nations, including the UK, Norway and Russia. Iceland's volcanic geology holds the potential for geothermal energy production.

India

Jan	1	Fr	New Year's Day	Sep	29	We	Dussehra Mela (2 days)
	19	Tu	Id Ul Fitr	Oct	2	Sa	Mahatma Gandhi's Birthday
	26	Tu	Republic Day	Nov	7	Su	Diwali
May	1	Sa	May Day	Dec	25	Sa	Christmas
Aug	15	Su	Independence Day				

Standard time: Zone 17½

- With almost 1 billion people, India's population is exceeded only by China. India encompasses many different cultures, each of which has distinct customs, languages and traditions. India's official holidays include Muslim (Id Ul Fitr), Hindu (Dussehra Mela, Diwali) and Christian (Christmas) festivals.

- The official languages are Hindi and English, but many other languages are spoken as well. As a former British colony, the English language is seen as a unifying factor in India. Many English-speaking Indians still use the polite phrases and linguistic patterns common to 19th century English.

- The traditional greeting among Indians is the *namaskar*. Upon meeting, each person raises his or her hands and holds them together—very much like Christians praying. The fingertips are raised approximately to the level of the chin. The entire motion is usually accompanied by a slight bow. Along with this gesture, a phrase of greeting is spoken by both persons. Hindus generally say the word *namaste*, which can be translated as "I salute the divine within you." Different ethnic and religious groups use different greeting phrases, but most use the same gesture.

- Indian men who do business with foreigners may offer to shake hands with men. Contact between persons of the same sex is common, and it is not unusual to see Indian men walking hand-in-hand. But public contact between the genders is rare, and men do not usually shake hands with women.

- Even when speaking in English, Indians often use indigenous counting systems for calculating large numbers. The two most common are the *lakh*, which is one hundred thousand, and the *crore*, which is ten million. Large figures in the Indian currency (the rupee) are always given in *lakhs* and *crores*.

Indonesia

Jan	1	Fr	New Year's Day	May	13	Th	Ascension of Christ
	19	Tu	Idul Fitri		30	Su	Waisak Day
	20	We	Idul Fitri	Jun	26	Sa	Birthday of Mohammad
Mar	18	Th	Seclusion Day	Aug	17	Tu	Independence Day
	28	Su	Idul Adha	Nov	6	Sa	Ascension of Mohammad
Apr	2	Fr	Good Friday	Dec	25	Sa	Christmas Day
	17	Sa	Moslem New Year				

Standard time: Zones 19, 20, 21
    Western (Sumatra, Java, Jakarta): Zone 19
    Northern and central (Bali, Kalimantan, Sulawesi, Nusatenggara): Zone 20
    Eastern (Maluku, Irianjaya): Zone 20

- The 200 million people of the Indonesian archipelago have diverse languages, religions and customs. Although Indonesia is often called "the world's largest Islamic nation," it also has substantial Christian and Hindu populations.

- Local businesses are concentrated in the hands of Indonesia's small Chinese population. However, in the past, little *international* business was accomplished without the participation of the relatives and friends of former President Suharto (who were mostly ethnic Indonesian). Suharto was forced to step down in 1998, but it remains to be seen if this will change.

Ireland

Jan	1	Fr	New Year's Day	Jun	7	Mo	Summer holiday
Mar	17	We	St. Patrick's Day	Aug	2	Mo	Summer holiday
Apr	2	Fr	Good Friday	Oct	25	Mo	October holiday
	5	Mo	Easter Monday	Dec	25	Sa	Christmas Day
May	3	Mo	May Day		26	Su	St. Stephen's Day

Standard time: Zone 12

- Punctuality has never been prized in Ireland. There is no shame to being a few minutes late to an appointment, or for an event to start late, or for a delivery date to be missed. To lose one's temper at such things would be impolite. A foreigner who becomes angry at such things will be accused of not understanding the Irish way of doing things. (Polite, repeated encouragements are more likely to get the desired result.)

- Peace efforts seem to be reducing the terrorist violence known as "The Troubles." Whether or not this continues, visiting businesspeople are rarely targeted. Moreover, this violence is largely restricted to neighboring *Northern* Ireland, which is part of the United Kingdom.

Israel

Feb	1	Mo	Tu B'Shevat	Jul	22	Th	Tisha B'Av
Mar	2	Tu	Purim	Sep	11	Sa	Rosh Hashana (first day)
Apr	1	Th	Passover (first day)		12	Su	Rosh Hashana (last day)
	7	We	Passover (last day)		20	Mo	Yom Kippur
	13	Tu	Holocaust Memorial Day		26	Su	Sukkot (first day)
	20	Tu	Memorial Day	Oct	1	Fr	Sukkot (last day)
	21	We	Independence Day		2	Sa	Simchat Torah
May	4	Th	Lag B'Omer	Dec	4	Sa	Hanukkah (first day)
	14	Fr	Jerusalem Day		11	Sa	Hanukkah (last day)
	21	Fr	Shavuot				

Standard time: Zone 14

- The workweek in Israel runs Sunday through Thursday. No business is conducted on the Jewish Sabbath, which begins at sundown every Friday and ends at sundown on Saturday.

- Israel has two official languages: Hebrew and Arabic. Many other languages are spoken, including English, French, Landino (the language of Sephardic Jews), Russian (from the many Russian Jews who have immigrated), and Yiddish (the language of Ashkenazi Jews). English is spoken by many in the business community.

- Both Hebrew and Arabic are written right-to-left, the opposite direction from English (which is written left-to-right). The back cover of an English-language magazine or report is the front cover of a Hebrew or Arabic one. Even if you do not translate your business materials into Hebrew, the back covers should be attractive, since this may be the first page a native-speaker of Hebrew looks at.

Italy

Jan	1	Fr	New Year's Day	Aug	15	Su	Assumption
	6	We	Epiphany	Sep	19	Su	St. Gennaro's Day (Naples)
Apr	4	Su	Easter Sunday	Nov	1	Mo	All Saints Day
	5	Mo	Easter Monday	Dec	7	Tu	St. Ambrose's Day (Milan)
	25	Su	Liberation Day		8	We	Immaculate Conception
	25	Su	St. Mark's Day (Venice)		25	Sa	Christmas Day
May	1	Sa	Labor Day		26	Su	St. Stephen's Day
Jun	29	Tu	St. Peter's Day (Rome)				

Standard time: Zone 13

- Although Italians are associated in the public mind with large families, Italy's birth rate has declined so rapidly that the population is not even renewing itself. In 1996, Italy's birth rate per 1,000 was just 9.2%, while the death rate per 1,000 was 9.5%—a net loss of 0.3%!

- Italians want their country to be considered the equal of other nations. While the Italian gross national product is impressive, it does not match that of Europe's leading nations. The Group of Five nations (the USA, Japan, the UK, France and Germany) was expanded to the Group of Seven (adding Italy and Canada) largely to fulfill Italian demands. This was little more than a face-saving gesture; the original Five still call the shots.

Jamaica

Jan	1	Fr	New Year's Day	Aug	1	Su	Emancipation Day
Feb	17	We	Ash Wednesday		6	Fr	Independence Day
Apr	2	Fr	Good Friday	Oct	18	Mo	National Heroes Day
	5	Mo	Easter Monday	Dec	25	Sa	Christmas Day
May	24	Mo	Labor Day		26	Su	Boxing Day

Standard time: Zone 7

- In business environments, a handshake is the usual greeting. In social situations, Jamaicans have several variations on the handshake. Jamaican men may touch each other's clenched fist as a sort of abbreviated handshake. Alternately, a handshake may evolve into a mock thumb-wrestling contest!

Japan

Jan	1	Fr	New Year's Day	May	5	We	Children's Day
	2	Sa	Bank Holiday	Jul	20	Tu	Marine Day
	3	Su	Bank Holiday	Sep	15	We	Respect for the Aged Day
	15	Fr	Adults' Day		23	Th	Autumnal Equinox Day
Feb	11	Th	National Foundation Day	Oct	10	Su	Health-Sports Day
Mar	21	Su	Vernal Equinox Day		11	Mo	Health-Sports Day observed
	22	Mo	Vernal Equinox Day observed	Nov	3	We	Culture Day
Apr	29	Th	Greenery Day		23	Tu	Labor Thanksgiving Day
May	3	Mo	Constitution Memorial Day	Dec	23	Th	Emperor's Birthday
	4	Tu	National Holiday		31	Fr	Bank Holiday

Standard time: Zone 21

- Always have your business card handy. Your card should be printed in Japanese on one side and in your own language on the other. The exchange of business cards is highly structured in Japan.

- Although all Japanese study English, few are proficient in verbal communications. Expect to engage an interpreter. When translating from Japanese into English, your interpreter might complete the translation before the speaker has finished. This is because most Japanese sentences quickly become predictable. To finish a sentence in Japanese in an unexpected manner would be considered impolite.

- Public displays of strong emotion are disliked by the Japanese. Someone who loses his or her temper at someone else brings shame and embarrassment upon both parties.

- In crowded trains and subways, riders are expected to keep their palms flat against their legs. This reduces the possibility that an accidental touch could be interpreted as a sexual advance.

Kazakhstan

Jan	1	Fr	New Year's Day	May	9	Su	Victory Day
	2	Sa	New Year's Day holiday	Aug	30	Mo	Constitution Day
Mar	8	Mo	International Women's Day	Oct	25	Mo	Republic Day
	22	Mo	Nauryz meyrami	Dec	16	Th	Independence Day
May	1	Sa	Labor Day				

Standard time: Zone 18

- The Kazakh Soviet Socialist Republic became the independent nation of Kazakhstan (also spelled *Kazakstan,* without the *h*) upon the dissolution of the USSR in 1991.

- The official language is Kazak. Ethnic Kazaks constitute less than half of the population. Over one-third of the population is ethnic Russian, but they are concentrated in Kazakhstan's north.

- Ethnic Kazaks are primarily Sunni Muslim. Although religion was discouraged under Soviet rule, Muslim practices are now flourishing. The traditional Muslim proscriptions should be observed: no alcohol, no pork or pig leather, no public contact between the sexes.

- Elders were traditionally revered among ethnic Kazaks. Respect should always be shown to the elderly. In the past, Muslim Kazak women lived under relatively few restrictions and played a strong role in the economy. It is unclear if this will continue; some fundamentalist Muslims are calling for more restrictions on women.

- Kazakhstan is blessed with many natural resources, and has been the focus of foreign investment, especially in the petroleum industry. Foreign control of Kazak resources is viewed with suspicion by many.

- The USSR constructed its main space launching center, the Baikonur Cosmodrome, in Kazakhstan. After the USSR broke up, this made the independent nation of Kazakhstan one of the few nations on Earth with space-launching capability! (However, the Kazak space center is still run primarily by Russian technicians.)

Korea (South)

Jan	1	Fr	New Year's Day	May	22	Sa	Buddha's Birthday
	2	Sa	New Year's holiday	Jun	6	Su	Memorial Day
Feb	14	Su	Lunar New Year's holiday	Jul	17	Sa	Constitution Day
	15	Mo	Lunar New Year's Day	Aug	15	Su	Liberation Day
	16	Tu	Lunar New Year's holiday	Sep	24	Fr	Harvest Festival holiday
	17	We	Lunar New Year's holiday		25	Sa	Harvest Festival
Mar	1	Mo	Independence Movement Day		26	Su	Harvest Festival holiday
Apr	5	Mo	Arbor Day	Oct	3	Su	National Foundation Day
May	5	We	Children's Day	Dec	25	Sa	Christmas Day

Standard time: Zone 21

- Citizens of the USA and Korea have different attitudes towards eye contact. In the US, someone who does not directly meet your gaze is often suspected of being untrustworthy. However, South Koreans find continued, intense eye contact to be aggressive and threatening. In general, South Koreans of equal status will meet each other's eyes about half the time. When two South Koreans who are of unequal status converse, the lower-ranking person will avert his or her eyes most of the time.

- In Korea's agricultural past, punctuality was not traditionally valued. Today it is becoming more important among the South Koreans. Foreigners are expected to be on time for all business appointments. Most Korean businesspeople will arrive within 10 or 15 minutes of the appointed time.

- Most South Koreans have three names. The surname is given first, followed by the two given names. For example, in the name Kim Hyong Sim, Kim is his surname, and he would be called Mr. Kim. (The most common surnames in Korea are Kim, Park and Lee.) Many families use one of the same given names for each member of a generation. Consequently, Mr. Kim's brothers and cousins might be named Kim Hyong Soo and Kim Hyong Min. Or they might share the second given name, such as Kim Young Sim and Kim Jae Sim. In English, the given names are sometimes hyphenated, so Kim Hyong Sim's name could be written as Kim Hyong-sim.

- Protocol is taken very seriously in South Korea. During a 1993 visit, US President Bill Clinton committed several blunders. Several times, he incorrectly referred to the wife of President Kim Young Sam as "Mrs. Kim." He forgot that married women in Korea keep their maiden names. President Kim's wife, Sohn Myong Suk, is correctly referred to as Madame Sohn.

- While Communist North Korea has languished economically, dynamic South Korea experienced tremendous growth since the end of the Korean War in 1953. In recent years, outsiders saw South Korea as one of Asia's "economic dragons," and a formidable competitor. While Koreans were proud of their accomplishments, many still saw themselves as a poor country scrambling to achieve economic stability. South Korea's boom halted with the massive economic dislocations of 1998. The economic crisis has added to Koreans' self-image as a poor nation in need of protective economic tariffs.

- Japan occupied Korea from 1910 to 1945. The Koreans suffered great hardships under the Japanese occupation. To this day, many Koreans retain bad feelings about the Japanese, and Japan is not a good topic of conversation among Koreans.

Kuwait

Jan	1	Fr	New Year's Day	Apr	17	Sa	Hijra New Year
	18	Mo	Eid Al-Fitr (3 days)	Jun	26	Sa	Prophet Mohammed's Birthday
Feb	25	Th	National Day	Nov	5	Fr	Prophet Mohammed's Ascension
	26	Fr	Liberation Day	Dec	10	Fr	Start of Ramadan (approx.)
Mar	28	Su	Eid Al-Adha (3 days)				

Standard time: Zone 15

- Kuwaiti men who deal with foreigners usually offer to shake hands with other men. Although Kuwaiti women do not have as much freedom as men, they make up a substantial portion of the workforce. Kuwaiti women do not traditionally shake hands. As in other Islamic countries, there is no physical contact between the sexes in public. However, if a Kuwaiti woman offers to shake hands, do so.

- The official language of Kuwait is Arabic. Classical Arabic (the language of the Koran) is revered by the Arab people. However, in daily life, people speak modern dialects of Arabic. Kuwaitis speak the dialect known as Gulf Arabic, which is shared by most of the people of the Arab peninsula. Gulf Arabic is mutually intelligible with that spoken by Egyptians and Palestinians. However, speakers of Gulf Arabic may have a difficult time communicating with speakers of the Arabic dialects used in Iraq or North Africa.

- English is widely spoken among Kuwaiti businessmen.

Madagascar

Jan	1	Fr	New Year's Day		May	25	Tu	African Unity Organization Day
Mar	29	Mo	Memorial Day		Jun	26	Sa	National Day
Apr	5	Mo	Easter Monday		Aug	15	Su	Assumption
May	1	Sa	Labor Day		Nov	1	Mo	All Saints Day
	13	Th	Ascension		Dec	25	Sa	Christmas
	24	Mo	Whit Monday					

Standard time: Zone 15

- As a former French colony, Madagascar's most widely spoken secondary language is French. English-speakers are uncommon. Malagasy is the national language, although the 1992 constitution does not designate any official languages.

- While there are substantial numbers of Christians, the majority of Malagasy follow traditional beliefs. These beliefs include an active relationship with the dead. Well-kept tombs can be seen everywhere.

- Experienced travelers to Madagascar recommend planning for the unexpected. Madagascar is a very poor nation, and many things seem on the verge of breaking down at any moment. One traveler told of a Madagascar Airlines flight which made 7 landings during a short commute, and never did get to its destination. Taxi drivers customarily coast downhill to save on gas.

- Madagascar is a signatory to the COMESA agreement, the Common Market for Eastern and Southern Africa. Still in its infancy, COMESA hopes to reduce trade barriers and eventually issue a common currency for use among its 21 member nations.

- Madagascar has suffered from natural disasters in recent years, ranging from drought to plagues of locusts. Since Madagascar contains many forms of plant and animal life found nowhere else on Earth, this is a matter of concern to biologists everywhere.

Malaysia

Jan	19	Tu	Raya Puasa	May	29	Sa	Wesak
	20	We	Raya Puasa	Jun	5	Sa	Birthday of Yang DiPertuan Agong
Feb	16	Tu	Chinese New Year		26	Sa	Prophet's Birthday
	17	We	Chinese New Year	Aug	31	Tu	National Day
Mar	28	Su	Raya Qurban	Nov	7	Su	Deepavali
Apr	17	Sa	Awal Muharam	Dec	25	Sa	Christmas
May	1	Sa	Labor Day				

Standard time: Zone 20

- Malaysia has three major ethnic groups (the Malay, the Chinese, and the Indians), as well as many smaller ones. Most of the international businesspeople are ethnic Chinese. However, government service is dominated by ethnic Malays.

- The official language is Bahasa Malaysian. All official materials must be written in this language. Bahasa Malaysian is mutually intelligible with the official language of Indonesia, which is called Bahasa Indonesia.

- The basic forms of address in Bahasa Malaysian are:

  Encik = Mr.
  Puan = Mrs.
  Cik = Miss

- Smiles are not necessarily displays of amusement in Malaysia. A smile is often used to hide embarrassment or confusion.

Mexico

Jan	1	Fr	New Year's Day	Oct	12	Tu	Columbus Day
Feb	5	Fr	Constitution Day	Nov	2	Tu	All Souls Day
Mar	21	Su	Juarez Birthday		20	Sa	Mexican Revolution
Apr	1	Th	Holy Thursday	Dec	12	Su	Our Lady of Guadalupe
	2	Fr	Good Friday		24	Fr	Christmas Eve
May	1	Sa	Labor Day		25	Sa	Christmas Day
	5	We	Puebla Battle		31	Fr	New Year's Eve
Sep	16	Th	Independence Day				

Standard time: Zone 4, 5, 6
    Baja California Norte (Tijuana) Zone 4
    Baja California Sur (Mazatlan): Zone 5
    Central and Western Mexico (Mexico City): Zone 6

- Mexico is the most populous Spanish-speaking nation in Latin America. Only Portuguese-speaking Brazil has more people (or a larger Gross National Product). Mexico is currently one of the three partners in the North American Free Trade Agreement, NAFTA.

- Mexico has had a complex historical relationship with many other countries. Much of the Southwestern USA was once part of Mexico. After achieving independence from Spain, the Mexican Empire claimed all of Central America down to the Panamanian border. For a brief time, Mexico ruled what is now Costa Rica, Nicaragua, Honduras, El Salvador, and Guatemala. Mexico's influence was not even limited to this continent; the Spanish Empire ruled the remote Philippines through Mexico.

- Citizens of the USA and Mexico have different attitudes towards eye contact. In the US, someone who does not directly meet your gaze is often suspected of being untrustworthy. Mexicans find continued, intense eye contact to be aggressive and threatening. Mexican business executives expect intermittent eye contact.

- Although the patterns of US-style business practices are becoming more common, Mexican business is still done on a personal basis. It can be difficult to get anything done without a network.

- The family is the single most important institution in Mexico. Because of this, nepotism is an accepted practice. Mexican executives generally put a higher importance on the best interest of their families than on the company they work for.

Morocco

Jan	1	Fr	New Year's Day	May	23	Su	National holiday
	11	Mo	National holiday	Jun	26	Sa	Prophet's Birthday
	19	Tu	Idul-Fitr	Jul	9	Fr	Youth Day
Mar	3	We	Throne Day	Aug	14	Sa	Oued-Ed-Dahab Day
Apr	18	Su	New Hijra Year		20	Fr	Revolution of the King and the People Day
	27	Tu	Idul-Adha (2 days)	Nov	6	Sa	Al-Massira Day
May	1	Sa	Labor Day		18	Th	Independence Day

Standard time: Zone 12

- Greetings are important in Morocco. A Moroccan greeting begins with a handshake, which may last much longer than the brief North American handshake. Traditionally, once the handshake is broken, each person touches his right hand to his chest. Some people may kiss their own right hand.

- Good friends and family are greeted with an embrace. Men may kiss each other once on each cheek. Moroccan women may kiss each other numerous times.

- Although Morocco is a Muslim country, contact between the genders is not strictly prohibited. Men and women often shake hands. However, a man should not offer to shake hands with a woman who is veiled.

- As in other Muslim countries, the left hand is considered unclean. Do not touch anyone or eat with your left hand.

Nepal

Jan	11	Mo	Prithvi Jayanti		Mar	25	Th	Chaitrastami
	22	Fr	Basanta Panchami			26	Fr	Ram Nawami
	30	Sa	Martyr's Day		Apr	14	We	Nepali New Year's Day
Feb	14	Su	Shiva Ratri		May	11	Tu	Buddha Jayanti[1]
	19	Fr	National Democracy Day		Sep	5	Su	Indra Jatra[1]
Mar	1	Mo	Fagu		Nov	9	Tu	Constitution Day[1]
	8	Mo	Women's Day		Dec	29	We	H.H. King's Birthday[1]
	17	We	Ghode Jatra					

1 Date is approximate.

Standard time: Zone 17 2/3

- The Nepalese people are generally very friendly. Some visitors find the attention they attract (and the consequent lack of privacy) to be disconcerting. Doors are not traditionally locked in Nepal when someone is present, and curious Nepalese are apt to enter at any time. A locked door—whether in a home or office—is viewed with suspicion.

- The traditional greeting in Nepal is *namaste*. Nepalese also say *namaste* upon departure. The word namaste can be translated as "I salute the divine within you."

- As is common in agricultural societies, the Nepalese tend to be casual about time and punctuality. Only in a few offices and government departments is punctuality given a priority. On the other hand, Nepalese folk beliefs which determine the most auspicious moment for important endeavors (such as weddings) can cause events to commence at an exact time.

- In Nepalese tradition, the head is considered sacred and the feet are considered unclean. Do not touch anyone on the head, not even to tousle the hair of a child. Do not touch anyone with your feet or shoes. Shoes are removed before entering most Nepalese homes or temples. Do not point at anyone with your feet or display the sole of your foot. (This proscription makes it difficult to sit with crossed legs!) Even stepping over another person is considered insulting.

- The Nepalese village of Lumbini is the reputed birthplace of Siddhartha Gautama, who became the Enlightened One—better known as the Buddha. Although Nepal's official religion is Hinduism, not Buddhism, the Royal Government of Nepal intends to develop this site. The government hopes to make Lumbini as important to Buddhist pilgrims as Mecca is to Muslims, or Jerusalem to Jews and Christians. To do so, massive improvements in infrastructure will need to be built around Lumbini.

Netherlands

Jan	1	Fr	New Year's Day	May	13	Th	Ascension
Apr	2	Fr	Good Friday		31	Mo	Whitmonday
	5	Mo	Easter Monday	Dec	25	Sa	Christmas Day
	30	Fr	Queen's Birthday		26	Su	Boxing Day
May	5	We	Liberation Day				

Standard time: Zone 13

- Although the Netherlands are associated with the Dutch Reformed Church, that is not the majority religion. The Roman Catholic Church has more than twice the membership of the Dutch Reformed Church. More Netherlanders consider themselves nonreligious or atheists than adhere to any single religion.

- Despite their enviable economic success, the Dutch do not brag; modesty and simplicity are hallmarks of Dutch culture. Thrift is respected while ostentation is frowned upon, leading many successful Dutch executives to live in houses in the same price range as their employees.

- Tolerance of others is considered a virtue. As far back as the 1500s, Jews fleeing the Spanish and Portuguese Inquisitions found refuge in the Netherlands. Later, Protestant Huguenots arrived, fleeing French persecution.

New Zealand

Jan	1	Fr	New Year's Day	Jun	7	Mo	Queen's Birthday
	4	Mo	New Year's holiday	Sep	27	Mo	Provincial Anniversary (Canterbury South)
	18	Mo	Provincial Anniversary (Southland)	Oct	22	Fr	Provincial Anniversary (Hawkes Bay)
	25	Mo	Provincial Anniversary (Wellington)		25	Mo	Labor Day
Feb	1	Mo	Provincial Anniversary (Auckland, Nelson)	Nov	1	Mo	Provincial Anniversary (Marlborough)
	6	Sa	Waitangi Day		12	Fr	Provincial Anniversary (Canterbury North)
Mar	8	Mo	Provincial Anniversary (Taranaki)		29	Mo	Provincial Anniversary (Chatham Islands, Westland)
	22	Mo	Provincial Anniversary (Otago)	Dec	25	Sa	Christmas Day
Apr	2	Fr	Good Friday		27	Mo	Christmas Day observed
	5	Mo	Easter Monday		28	Tu	Boxing Day observed
	25	Su	ANZAC Day				

Standard time: Zone 24

- Although there are similarities between New Zealanders (colloquially known as *Kiwis*, after their national bird) and Australians (*Aussies*), considerable rivalry exists between the two nations. *Kiwis* do not like being mistaken for *Aussies*, or vice-versa.

- Punctuality is considered important in New Zealand. Businesspeople who are late to meetings are viewed negatively.

- Perhaps because the Maori constitute over 15% of New Zealand's population, they have not been as marginalized as other indigenous peoples. The Maori remain an important part of New Zealand's cultural and political life, and some Maori terms are used by English-speaking Kiwis.

- The USA, Australia and New Zealand are signatories to the ANZUS mutual defense treaty, signed in 1951. However, New Zealand later declared itself a "nuclear free zone." Since the USA does not confirm which of its warships are carrying nuclear weapons, this has effectively barred all large US Navy vessels from New Zealand waters. This has been a long-standing matter of dispute between the USA and New Zealand.

- Despite the differences between the USA and New Zealand over nuclear weapons, in December 1998 New Zealand agreed to acquire 28 US F-16 fighter planes. The fighters were originally part of an order from Pakistan, but, after accepting the money, the USA declined to deliver the planes after Pakistan began to develop nuclear weapons. (Following the lead of India, Pakistan tested a thermonuclear device in May of 1998.) New Zealand will take the fighters on a 10-year lease-buy agreement for about US$105 million. The money is expected to go to Pakistan, which had already paid the US for the fighters.

Nicaragua

Jan	1	Fr	New Year's Day	Aug	1	Su	Festival of Santo Domingo
Apr	1	Th	Holy Thursday	Sep	14	Tu	Battle of San Jacinto
	2	Fr	Good Friday		15	We	Independence Day
May	1	Sa	Labor Day	Nov	2	Tu	All Souls Day
	30	Su	Mother's Day	Dec	8	We	Immaculate Conception
Jul	19	Mo	Sandinista Revolution Day		25	Sa	Christmas Day

Standard time: Zone 6

- The Nicaraguans call themselves *Nicas* or *Pinolleros*.

- Nicaraguans are fiercely patriotic and fond of debate. They hate being mistaken for any of their neighbors—especially their prosperous neighbors to the south, the Costa Ricans.

- Nicaraguans are generally informal. Greetings and introductions tend to be casual. The people dress informally—suits and ties are not required on men, and high heels are uncommon on women. Casual dress is appropriate for Nicaragua's climate, which is uncomfortably hot all year long.

- Hurricane Mitch devastated much of Nicaragua in late 1998. Damage to its infrastructure and agriculture has been estimated at US$1 billion—about half of Nicaragua's annual GNP. Recovery will be difficult unless Nicaragua receives debt relief; in 1998 its foreign debt was roughly US$6 billion.

- Central America has frequently seen intervention by the US military. However, only Nicaragua has suffered occupation at the hands of a private mercenary army from the USA. The bizarre invasion of Nicaragua by US adventurer William Walker is unique in Central American history. From 1855 to 1857, Walker and his 56 mercenaries held much of Nicaragua.

- Despite years of political upheaval, Nicaragua has a vibrant cultural life, spanning literature, art and theater. Many of Nicaragua's writers have spent years away from their home country, either in exile or to seek broader opportunities. Poetry is especially popular—Nicaraguans often claim that their country has more poets (per capita) than any country in the world.

Nigeria

Jan	1	Fr	New Year's Day	May	1	Sa	Labor Day
	19	Tu	Eid-El-Fitr (2 days)	Jun	26	Sa	Eid-El-Maulud
Mar	28	Su	Eid-El-Kabir (2 days)	Oct	1	Fr	National Day
Apr	2	Fr	Good Friday	Dec	25	Sa	Christmas Day
	5	Mo	Easter Monday		26	Su	Boxing Day

Standard time: Zone 13

- Unfortunately, Nigeria is known as the world's capital of mail-order fraud. Canadian officials estimate that Canadians have lost over US$1 million to Nigerian fraud. Estimates for the USA are far higher; one US citizen alone lost US$2 million. The Nigerian government has been of little help in stopping this situation. Occasionally, a US national who goes to Nigeria to follow up on these frauds is threatened or illegally held until he agrees to pay a large sum.

- Although the practice is dying out, do not be surprised to see Nigerians with geometric scars on their face or body. In the past, traditional scars identified specific clans and tribes.

Norway

Jan	1	Fr	New Year's Day	May	17	Mo	Constitution Day
Mar	28	Su	Palm Sunday		13	Th	Ascension Day
Apr	1	Th	Maundy Thursday		23	Su	Whitsun
	2	Fr	Good Friday		24	Mo	Whitmonday
	4	Su	Easter Sunday	Dec	25	Sa	Christmas Day
	5	Mo	Easter Monday		26	Su	Boxing Day
May	1	Sa	Labor Day				

Standard time: Zone 13

- Modern Norway has been an independent nation only since 1905. Before that, it passed back and forth between Danish and Swedish ownership.

- Norwegians tend to be more informal than other Scandinavians (especially the Swedes, whom they generally consider stuffy.)

- Many observers consider the Norwegians to be the least punctual people in Northern Europe. A 15-minute delay is not uncommon.

- Norwegian businesspeople are sometimes uncomfortable communicating in writing, especially in a foreign language. Many prefer to do business by telephone rather than by letter. When writing is necessary, it will often be as short as possible: a brief fax, telex or e-mail message suffices.

Pakistan

Jan	19	Tu	Eid-ul-Fitr (3 days)	Aug	14	Sa	Independence Day
Mar	23	Tu	Pakistan Day	Sep	6	Mo	Defense of Pakistan Day
	28	Su	Eid-ul-Azha (3 days)		11	Sa	Anniversary of the Death of Quaid-e-Azam
Apr	8	Th	Muharram (2 days)	Dec	25	Sa	Christmas
May	1	Sa	May Day		31	Sa	Bank holiday

Standard time: Zone 17

- Monsoon season runs from May until August. The best time of year to make a business trip to Pakistan is between October and April.

- Men shake hands with other men in Pakistan. Women do not usually shake hands with other women, and there is little contact between the genders in public.

- Gesturing with a closed fist is offensive in Pakistan.

- Pakistan is a predominantly Muslim country and traditional beliefs prevail.

Panama

Jan	1	Fr	New Year's Day	Aug	15	Su	Assumption
	9	Sa	National Mourning	Nov	3	We	Independence from Colombia
Feb	15	Mo	Carnival Monday		4	Th	Flag Day
	16	Tu	Carnival		10	We	First Announcement of Independence
	17	We	Ash Wednesday		28	Su	Independence from Spain
Apr	1	Th	Holy Thursday	Dec	8	We	Mothers' Day
	2	Fr	Good Friday		24	Fr	Christmas Eve
	3	Sa	Holy Saturday		25	Sa	Christmas Day
May	1	Sa	Labor Day		31	Sa	New Year's Eve

Standard time: Zone 7

- Urban white Panamanians hold most of the country's wealth and power. They are nicknamed *Los rabiblancos* (which means *whitetails*). Many of them speak English as well as Spanish. They are a separate group from the rural landowners, who never achieved the political influence which is characteristic of agricultural barons elsewhere in Central America.

- When Spain ruled Latin America, Panama was an important transshipment point for African slaves being sent to South America, and the country has a substantial black population today. This segment of the black population has lived in Panama for hundreds of years; they speak Spanish and are culturally Hispanicized. A second population of blacks came from Caribbean islands to work on the railroads and the Canal. Their origin in the Antilles led to the nickname *antillanos*, and many of them continue to speak English rather than Spanish.

- Panama is the only nation with a Canal linking the Atlantic and Pacific Oceans. The Panama Canal remains one of the wonders of the modern world. It is also a central issue in the lives of many Panamanians, who want Panama to own the Canal and the Canal Zone, but fear the loss of US expertise and money.

- Many Panamanians have nicknames. Even powerful politicians are often referred to by their nicknames. Dictator Manuel Antonio Noriega was known as *la Piña* (*the Pineapple*) due to his pock-marked complexion. His successor as President, the pleasant and rotund Guillermo Endara, was called *Pan de Dulce* (*Honey Bun*)!

- Although its distribution of wealth is very unequal, Panama remains the wealthiest Central American nation, in large part due to the Canal and US investment. (Mexico is wealthier, but it is considered part of North America, not Central America.)

Paraguay

Jan	1	Fr	New Year's Day	Jun	12	We	Peace with Bolivia
Mar	1	Mo	Heroes' Day	Aug	15	Su	Foundation of Asuncion
Apr	1	Th	Holy Thursday	Sep	29	We	Victory of Boqueron Battle
	2	Fr	Good Friday	Dec	8	We	Immaculate Conception
May	1	Sa	Labor Day		25	Sa	Christmas Day
	15	Sa	Independence Day				

Standard time: Zone 8

- Paraguay is one of two landlocked nations in South America. (Bolivia is the other one.) Until the advent of trucks and air transport, Paraguayans transported most of their goods by river.

- Paraguay is the only Latin American nation with two official languages: Spanish and Guaraní (an Amerindian language). However, virtually all businesspeople speak Spanish.

- Paraguay is known as the smuggling capital of South America. Huge amounts of counterfeit goods—worth as much as US$10 billion—enter the continent via Paraguay. Copyright infringement is a given in Paraguay. Much of the smuggling goes through Paraguay's *Ciudad del Este* Free Trade Zone.

- *Paraguayan tea,* also known as *mate* (pronounced *"mah-tay"*) is a popular drink served in Paraguay, Uruguay, and Argentina. It is prepared from the *yerba mate* leaf (*Ilex paraguayensis*), and, like coffee and tea, it contains caffeine. Visitors are often invited to sample *mate*, and there is a ritual to the process. Only one container (usually a decorated gourd) is used, no matter how many people are being served. The *cebador* (server) fills the gourd with chopped *yerba* leaves, then pours hot water into the gourd. The gourd is then handed to the first drinker, who sips the mixture through a silver straw. After the gourd is drained, it is returned to the *cebador*, who then refills it with hot water and hands the gourd to the next drinker.

- Paraguay has one of the warmest climates in the Americas. Paraguayans are not typically known for being driven businesspeople. Even commerce is conducted at a languid pace, and businesses often close early. Some visitors find the Paraguayan character to be refreshingly straightforward, relaxed and unpretentious.

Peru

Jan	1	Fr	New Year's Day	Jul	29	Th	Independence Day holiday
Apr	1	Th	Holy Thursday	Aug	30	Mo	St. Rosa of Lima
	2	Fr	Good Friday	Oct	8	Fr	Battle of Angamos
May	1	Sa	Labor Day	Nov	1	Mo	All Saints Day
Jun	29	Tu	Sts. Peter and Paul's Day	Dec	8	We	Immaculate Conception
Jul	28	We	Independence Day holiday		25	Sa	Christmas Day

Standard time: Zone 7

- Peru has always been a highly stratified society, with a wealthy oligarchy ruling over poor mestizos and even poorer Indians. The Amerindians constitute over half the population, followed by mestizos (persons of mixed European and Amerindian heritage) and whites. There is also a small community of Japanese immigrants, from which the current President, Alberto Fujimori, has descended.

- Peru has had difficult relations with its neighbors. Peru lost some valuable southern territory to Chile in the last century, and its border dispute with Ecuador broke out into fighting in early 1995.

- Peru now has three official languages: Spanish, plus the Amerindian languages Quechua and Aymara. All executives will speak Spanish, and some will speak English as well. Many Peruvian Indians are bilingual in Spanish and their native language. Only in the most remote areas are the Indians unfamiliar with Spanish.

- Although terrorist groups such as the Shining Path (Sendero Luminoso) and Túpac Amaru receive worldwide publicity, their actions do not generally affect the international business traveler. (The 1996 seizure of the Japanese Embassy in Lima by the Túpac Amaru Revolutionary Movement was an anomaly.) The cocaine industry has more influence on international business, due to its high profitability, inherent violence and government efforts to limit it. Peruvians grow more than half of the world's coca crop. The law enforcement agencies of many nations monitor the Peruvian drug traffic. Consequently, innocent business travelers to Peru may find police attention focused on them.

- The greatest threat to foreign travelers in Peru is not cholera outbreaks, terrorism, or earthquakes: it's altitude sickness. Lima is near sea level, but other popular destinations (such as Cuzco and the area around Lake Titicaca) are high enough to cause this illness. Anyone can be struck by altitude sickness, and rest is the only sure cure. Be aware that Peruvian folk remedies for the sickness usually contain coca leaves. (Coca leaves, which are chewed by many Amerindians, are legal in Peru. Cocaine itself is highly illegal.)

Philippines

Jan	1	Fr	New Year's Day	Aug	29	Su	National Heroes Day
Apr	1	Th	Holy Thursday	Nov	1	Mo	All Saints Day
	2	Fr	Good Friday		30	Tu	Bonifacio Day
	9	Fr	Araw Ng Kagitingan	Dec	25	Sa	Christmas Day
May	1	Sa	Labor Day		30	Th	Rizal Day
Jun	12	Sa	Independence Day		31	Fr	New Year's Eve

Standard time: Zone 20

- Appointments may be scheduled up to one month prior to your arrival in the Philippines.

- Titles are important to Filipinos, so every effort should be made to learn the correct forms of address. Filipinos consider titles so important that executives are sometimes rewarded with new titles instead of raises.

- Do not expect Filipinos to wait in neat lines in public places. Typically, Filipinos merge into a tight crowd, with everyone pushing towards the front. Orderly lines have a negative image, reminding Filipinos of the Japanese occupation during the Second World War, when the Japanese enforced queues at gunpoint.

Poland

Jan	1	Fr	New Year's Day	Aug	15	Su	Assumption
Apr	5	Mo	Easter Monday	Nov	1	Mo	All Saints Day
May	1	Sa	Labor Day		11	Th	Independence Day
	3	Mo	Constitution Day	Dec	25	Sa	Christmas Day
Jun	3	Th	Corpus Christi		26	Su	Christmas holiday

Standard time: Zone 13

- The Polish workday typically starts early. Factories may open at 6 AM; offices usually open between 7:30 and 8 AM. Appointments scheduled for 8 AM are not uncommon.

- The typical Polish honorifics are:

  Mr. = Pan (pronounced "pahn")
  Mrs. = Pani (pronounced "pah-nee")
  Miss = Panna (pronounced "pah-nah")

- Poles pride themselves on their hospitality. Foreigners (even business travelers) are often invited home for dinner.

- Business negotiations are often conducted by teams. A high-ranking person from your company must put in an appearance (at the very least) to show that your intent is serious.

Portugal

Jan	1	Fr	New Year's Day	Aug	15	Su	Assumption
Feb	16	Tu	Mardi Gras	Oct	5	Tu	Republic Day
Apr	2	Fr	Good Friday	Nov	1	Mo	All Saints Day
	25	Su	Liberty Day	Dec	1	We	Independence Day
May	1	Sa	Labor Day		8	We	Immaculate Conception
Jun	3	Th	Corpus Christi		24	Fr	Christmas Eve
	10	Th	Camoes-Portugal Day		25	Sa	Christmas Day
	13	Su	St. Anthony				

Standard time: Zone 11, 12, 13
    Azores: Zone 11
    Madeira: Zone 12
    Mainland Portugal: Zone 13

- Although Portugal is often thought of as a Mediterranean country, this is not geographically correct. Portugal is not on the Mediterranean Sea—its only coastline faces the Atlantic Ocean. That, plus its highly-navigable rivers (which empty into the Atlantic), tended to give the Portuguese people an outward orientation, focused away from the Mediterranean. In Portugal's heyday, the focus was aimed at the spice trade of the Indies, via the Eastward route around Africa.

- The Portuguese have a tradition of delegating hard or distasteful labor to others. Even aboard Portuguese warships during the height of the age of exploration, the artillerymen (a skilled but dangerous occupation) tended to be German or Flemish mercenaries.

- Although Portugal developed as a seafaring nation (and sailing is subject to the unremitting mercy of time and tide), punctuality was not a traditional priority. Although some attitudes have changed, there is still a casual attitude towards time. Foreigners are expected to be punctual for business appointments, but Portuguese may or may not be prompt.

- The Portuguese are not as physically demonstrative in public as either the Spanish or the Italians.

- Until recently, Portugal remained one of the last major colonial powers. Portugal's African colonies of Angola and Mozambique—established back in the 1500s—were only lost in 1974. Consequently, Portugal still has close ties with Africa, and there are many refugees from these colonies residing in Portugal.

Puerto Rico

Jan	1	Fr	New Year's Day	Jul	21	We	Muñoz-Rivera's Birthday
	6	We	Epiphany		25	Su	Constitution Day
	13	We	Hostos' Birthday		28	We	Barbosa's Birthday
	18	Mo	Martin Luther King Jr. Day	Sep	6	Mo	Labor Day
Feb	15	Mo	President's Day	Oct	11	Mo	Columbus Day
Mar	22	Mo	Emancipation Day	Nov	11	Th	Veterans Day
Apr	2	Fr	Good Friday		19	Fr	Discovery of Puerto Rico
	21	We	De Diego's Birthday		25	Th	Thanksgiving
May	31	Mo	Memorial Day	Dec	25	Sa	Christmas Day
Jul	4	Su	Independence Day				

Standard time: Zone 8

- The official language of Puerto Rico is Spanish, although English is widely spoken.

- By a narrow margin, Puerto Ricans voted in 1998 to continue their special commonwealth status. In future elections, it is expected that Puerto Ricans will vote either for independence or to petition for statehood in the USA.

- While Puerto Rico is a US Commonwealth and overrun with US business interests, it still boasts a predominantly Latino culture.

- Spanish is commonly spoken in meetings, although English can usually be accommodated.

- Relationships are key for opening doors.

- Variations from continental US taxes, holiday schedules, personnel law, etc., should be considered.

Romania

Jan	1	Fr	New Year's Day	May	1	Sa	Labor Day
	2	Sa	New Year's Day holiday	Dec	1	We	National Day
Apr	11	Su	Easter		25	Sa	Christmas Day
	12	Mo	Easter Monday		26	Su	Boxing Day

Standard time: Zone 14

- Romanians shake hands often: when they are introduced, when they depart, and even when they meet again on the same day.

- The Romanian elite has always traveled and studied abroad. Paris is the favorite destination, and many French customs and habits are followed by upper-class Romanians.

- Romanians have reputations as hard bargainers. One useful technique is to delineate the limits of what your negotiators can and cannot do. This should be done at the beginning of a meeting.

- Romanians also have reputations as risk-takers. Unpredictability, spontaneity, and boldness are considered part of the Romanian character. So is their sense of humor, which includes a fine appreciation of the absurd.

Russian Federation

Jan	1	Fr	New Year's Day	May	9	Su	Victory Day
	7	Th	Christmas Day	Jun	12	Sa	Independence Day
Mar	8	Mo	International Women's Day	Aug	22	Su	Day of the Russian Federation State Flag
May	1	Sa	Labor Day	Nov	7	Su	Day of Accord and Conciliation
	2	Su	Labor Day holiday	Dec	12	Su	Constitution Day

Standard time: Zones 15, 16, 17, 18, 19, 20, 21, 22, 23, 24, 1
   Western European (Leningrad, Moscow): Zone 15
   Central European (Rostov, Baku): Zone 16
   Eastern European (Sverdlovsk): Zone 17
   Western Siberia (Alma Ata): Zone 18; (Novosibirsk) Zone 19; (Irkutsk) Zone 10
   Central Siberia (Yakutsk): Zone 21; (Vladivostok) Zone 22
   Eastern Siberia (Magadan): Zone 23; (Petropavlovsk) Zone 24 (Uelen) Zone 1

- "Time is money" is a concept alien to Russia. Although things are changing, do not expect punctuality.

- During business discussions, Russians dislike compromise. To compromise is seen as failure.

- Russians are not afraid to show emotion during negotiations. Shouting and walking out are considered valid negotiating tools.

- Russian business society was never oriented towards quick action. Traditionally, issues are discussed at great length before any action is taken.

- Travel in Russia can be quite difficult. In addition to the harsh weather and the country's deteriorating infrastructure, the Russian Federation is the world's largest nation. Russia is so huge that it spans 11 time zones.

Saudi Arabia

Jan	12	Tu	Eid Al-Fitr (first day)	Apr	2	Fr	Eid Al-Adha (last day)
	22	Fr	Eid Al-Fitr (last day)	Sep	23	Th	Saudi National Day
Mar	22	Mo	Eid Al-Adha (first day)				

Standard time: Zone 15

- The Islamic proscriptions against alcohol, pork and pornography are tightly enforced in Saudi Arabia. Foreigners found in possession of any of these are subject to arrest and/or deportation. (Remember that the avoidance of pork includes avoiding pig leather.)

- Don't expect appointments in Saudi Arabia to start on time. Traditional Arab business meetings are rarely private. Typically, you will be ushered into a room with several people and one person will act as host. He will probably make extensive inquiries into your health and journey before starting to talk about business. The other people in the room may or may not be introduced. Your host can interrupt your sales pitch at any time to converse with others in the room. The others in the room might pay attention to your pitch, or they may carry on conversations of their own. If a new person arrives, your host might ask you to repeat all or part of your presentation. You may have no idea who the decision maker is (although it's probably an older man who watches everything yet says nothing). Finally, you will be served coffee, encouraging things will be said (but no contracts signed), and your appointment is over.

- The government of Saudi Arabia places extreme restrictions on women. Women may not drive and are barred from many occupations. Their interactions with men are supposed to be limited to relatives and servants.

- Despite the heat, both men and women must dress modestly in Saudi Arabia. Most of the body must be covered; shorts or tight-fitting clothes are not acceptable. Persons who fail to cover enough skin are liable to feel the camel-hair whips of the Matawain (the religious police) on the offending body part. Being a foreigner affords no protection from the Matawain.

Senegal

Jan	1	Fr	New Year's Day	May	24	Mo	Whit Monday
Apr	4	Su	National Day/Easter	Aug	15	Su	Assumption
	5	Mo	Easter Monday	Nov	1	Mo	All Saints Day
May	1	Sa	Labor Day	Dec	25	Sa	Christmas
	13	Th	Ascension				

Standard time: Zone 12

- A former colony of France, French is the official language of Senegal. (Most Senegalese speak an indigenous language called Wolof.) In addition to maintaining close relations with France, Senegal is receiving substantial aid from Taiwan.

- Men shake hands upon arrival and departure. Hands may remain gently clasped for a long time in Senegal, while pleasantries are exchanged. Greetings include inquiries to the health and status of every family member. Senegalese men usually offer their hand to a foreign woman. However, foreign men should not shake hands with a Senegalese woman unless she offers her hand. Many Senegalese women are involved in business—some of them at a very high level.

- Most Senegalese are Muslim. As in other Muslim countries, the left hand is considered unclean. Always use your right hand to eat. Use your right hand in preference to your left, but both hands may be used to handle something heavy.

- Senegal has had conflicts with its neighboring countries, especially when large numbers of refugees try to enter Senegal. In June of 1998, fighting broke out between Senegal and Guinea-Bissau.

Singapore

Jan	1	Fr	New Year's Day	May	29	Sa	Vesak Day
	19	Tu	Hari Raya Puasa	Aug	9	Mo	National Day
Feb	16	Tu	Chinese New Year (2 days)	Nov	7	Su	Deepavali
Mar	28	Su	Hari Raya Haji		8	Mo	Deepavali observed
Apr	2	Fr	Good Friday	Dec	25	Sa	Christmas Day
May	1	Sa	Labor Day				

Standard time: Zone 20

- Singapore has three major ethnic groups: the Chinese, the Malay, and the Indians. Most of the international businesspeople are ethnic Chinese.

- To unify these different ethnic groups, Singapore has adopted English as an official language (along with Mandarin Chinese, Bahasa Malaysia and Tamil). English provides a medium of communication between ethnic groups—including the Chinese, who include speakers of several mutually-unintelligible Chinese dialects.

- Although English is widely spoken among businesspeople and government employees, sentences may be constructed using Chinese grammatical patterns. For example, Chinese questions often end with the phrase "yes/no?"—which sounds demanding and harsh when spoken in English.

- While Singapore is an excellent place to do business, visitors should remember that it has a draconian legal code. Laws prohibiting littering, spitting, chewing gum, jaywalking, and smoking in public places are all enforced. The fine for failing to flush a public toilet after use is US$150.

Slovak Republic

Jan	1	Fr	New Year's Day	Aug	29	Su	Slovak National Uprising
	6	We	Epiphany	Sep	1	We	Constitution Day
Apr	2	Fr	Good Friday		15	We	Seven Sorrows of Virgin Mary
	5	Mo	Easter Monday	Nov	1	Mo	All Saints Day
May	1	Sa	Labor Day	Dec	24	Fr	Christmas Eve
	8	Sa	Victory Day		25	Sa	Christmas Day
Jul	5	Mo	Sts. Cyril and Methodius		26	Su	St. Stephen's Day

Standard time: Zone 13

- Until the breakup of Czechoslovakia in 1993, the Slovak people have never had the power of self-determination. They typically saw their heritage as one of powerlessness and victimization.

- Unlike the Czechs, religion is considered part of the Slovak national identity. The vast majority of Slovaks are Roman Catholics.

- Although the Slovaks have a good sense of humor, business is seen as serious. Jokes and laughter are inappropriate during business discussions.

- Not only is the Slovak language mutually intelligible with Czech, it can be understood by the speakers of many other Slavic languages.

South Africa

Jan	1	Fr	New Year's Day	Jun	16	We	Youth Day
Mar	21	Su	Human Rights Day	Aug	9	Mo	National Women's Day
	22	Mo	Human Rights Day observed	Sep	24	Fr	Heritage Day
Apr	2	Fr	Good Friday	Dec	16	Th	Day of Reconciliation
	5	Mo	Family Day		25	Sa	Christmas Day
	27	Tu	Freedom Day		26	Su	Day of Goodwill
May	1	Sa	Workers' Day		27	Mo	Day of Goodwill observed

Standard time: Zone 14

- Under the new constitution, South Africa now has a plethora of official languages. In addition to English and Afrikaans, they include Ndebele, Pedi (North Sotho), Sotho (South Sotho), Swazi, Tsonga, Tswana (West Sotho), Venda, Xhosa, and Zulu.

- While each of the many cultures of South Africa has its own customs, the majority of international executives are native speakers of either English or Afrikaans.

- South African executives are skilled negotiators, but they generally do not like to play hardball. A businessperson who gloats over crushing his or her competitors is not appreciated. The ideal business deal among English and Afrikaans is a "win-win situation." However, this may not be true of businesspeople from other ethnic groups, especially the Chinese and Malay communities.

- English and Afrikaans executives often invite visitors to a barbecue. A barbecue, called a *braaivleis* (Afrikaans for "roasted meat") is a social occasion—business will not be discussed. Guests often bring something to contribute to a *braaivleis.* Ask what you can provide, although as a foreign guest your offer may be declined.

- When lightning strikes in South Africa, it is a common occurrence. Use a surge suppressor for your laptop computers and modems.

Spain

Jan	1	Fr	New Year's Day	Aug	15	Su	Assumption
	6	We	Epiphany	Sep	11	Sa	Catalonia Day
Mar	19	Fr	St. Joseph's Day	Oct	12	Tu	Spanish National Day
Apr	1	Th	Holy Thursday	Nov	1	Mo	All Saints Day
	2	Fr	Good Friday	Dec	6	Mo	Constitution Day
	3	Sa	Holy Saturday		8	We	Immaculate Conception
	5	Mo	Easter Monday		25	Sa	Christmas Day
May	1	Sa	Labor Day		26	Su	St. Stephen's Day
Jul	25	Su	National Day of Galicia				

Standard time: Zone 12, 13
Canary Islands: Zone 12
Mainland Spain: Zone 13

- Castilian Spanish is the official language, but several autonomous regions have their own languages. Most of these are regional variations of Spanish, ranging from Gallego (which is similar to Portuguese) in Galicia to Catalan in Catalonia. The exception is the Basque language, which is totally unrelated to Spanish (or any other known language). The Basques call their language Euskera; the Basque region is Euskadi.

- A foreigner, trained in Castilian Spanish, may not be able to understand all of the regional variations of Spanish, although regional speakers generally understand Castilian.

- Time unfolds differently on the Iberian peninsula. Very little seems to take place precisely at its appointed time.

- Meals in Spain are eaten late. The midday meal usually waits until 2 PM, and the evening meal doesn't start before 9 PM. To tide them over, many people enjoy an early evening snack in a *tapas* bar—a uniquely Spanish institution.

- Personal relationships determine an executive's power in Spain. Job titles do not necessarily reflect the true importance or power of individual executives.

- Long-term planning is not a traditional strength of Spanish organizations. The prevailing philosophy is that the future is unknowable, so detailed planning is futile. Emphasis is placed on how well executives improvise when unexpected crises occur.

Jan	1	Fr	Duruthu Full Moon Poya Day	May	29	Sa	Vesak Full Moon Poya Day
	15	Fr	Tamil Thai Pongal Day		30	Su	Day after Vesak Full Moon Poya Day
	19	Tu	Id-Ul-Fitr	Jun	27	Su	Maulid al-Nabi
	31	Su	Navam Full Moon Poya Day		28	Mo	Poson Full Moon Poya Day
Feb	4	Th	National Day	Jul	28	We	Esala Full Moon Poya Day
	14	Su	Maha Sivarathri Day	Aug	26	Th	Nikini Full Moon Poya Day
Mar	1	Mo	Medin Full Moon Poya Day	Sep	25	Sa	Binara Full Moon Poya Day
	29	Mo	Idul Allah	Oct	24	Su	Vap Full Moon Poya Day
	31	We	Bak Full Moon Poya Day	Nov	7	Su	Deepavali Festival Day
Apr	2	Fr	Good Friday		22	Mo	Il Full Moon Poya Day
	13	Tu	Day Prior to Sinhala and Tamil New Year	Dec	22	We	Unduwap Full Moon Poya Day
	14	We	Sinhala and Tamil New Year Day		25	Sa	Christmas Day
May	1	Sa	May Day				

Standard time: Zone 17½

- Sri Lanka has two official languages: Sinhala and Tamil. English is commonly used by the business community. Some older and younger Sri Lankan citizens also speak English. Middle-aged Sri Lankans did not learn English because of the "Sinhala Only" laws in place from 1956 through the late 1980s.

- There has been considerable conflict between the Sinhalese and Tamil communities. Such conflict rarely affects foreigners. One way to tell the groups apart is by their surnames. Sinhalese names usually end in a vowel, while Tamil names usually end in a consonant—especially the letters "n" and "m."

- The rhetorical phrase "What to do?" is often heard from Sri Lankans during deliberations. It usually indicates that no decision will be made at that time.

- Sri Lankans' conception of time is not the same as that of Westerners. Punctuality has not traditionally been considered a virtue.

Sweden

Jan	1	Fr	New Year's Day	May	24	Mo	Whit Monday
	6	We	Epiphany	Jun	26	Sa	Midsummer day
Apr	2	Fr	Good Friday	Nov	6	Sa	All Saints Day
	4	Su	Easter Sunday	Dec	24	Fr	Christmas Eve
	5	Mo	Easter Monday		25	Sa	Christmas Day
May	1	Sa	Labor Day		26	Su	Boxing Day
	13	Th	Ascension Day		31	Fr	New Year's Eve
	23	Su	Whit Sunday				

Standard time: Zone 13

- Swedes traditionally find outward displays of emotion to be distasteful. While this trait is common to all Scandinavians, it is especially pronounced in Sweden. Sales techniques which use hype or high enthusiasm are rarely successful in Sweden.

- Swedes can sometimes be differentiated from Danes or Norwegians by the spelling of their last names. Many Swedish surnames usually end in -ON, while Danish and Norwegian surnames tend to end in -EN. Consequently, someone named *Olson* or *Nelson* or *Jenson* is probably Swedish, while *Olsen* or *Nelsen* or *Jensen* is usually Danish or Norwegian.

- Swedish executives have a reputation as good negotiators, who can remain polite even while driving a hard bargain. They also consider quality to be one of the most important issues.

- Old, established firms have a cachet in some countries, but don't expect that to impress the Swedes. The Swedes have been engaged in business for centuries. Stora Kopparberg (now known as Stora-Great) began as a copper mining firm over 700 years ago, and has records dating back to the year 1288!

Switzerland

Jan	1	Fr	New Year's Day	May	24	Mo	Whit Monday
	2	Sa	Berchtoldstag Day[1]	Jun	3	Th	Corpus Christi[1]
	6	We	Epiphany[1]	Aug	1	Su	National Day
Feb	17	We	Ash Wednesday[1]		15	Su	Assumption[1]
Mar	28	Su	Palm Sunday[1]	Sep	20	Mo	Thanksgiving Monday[1]
Apr	2	Fr	Good Friday	Nov	1	Mo	All Saints' Day[1]
	4	Su	Easter Sunday	Dec	8	We	Immaculate Conception[1]
	5	Mo	Easter Monday		24	Fr	Christmas Eve[1]
May	1	Sa	Labor Day[1]		25	Sa	Christmas Day
	13	Th	Ascension		26	Su	Boxing Day
	23	Su	Whit Sunday		31	Fr	New Year's Eve[1]

1. Some cantons (states) only; some cantons half day only

Standard time: Zone 13

- Switzerland has three official languages: German, French and Italian. Each of these groups has its own cultural identity with its own customs and ways of doing business.

- Punctuality, organization and planning are important to most Swiss executives. Be on time to all appointments. Your presentations should be well-organized with data to back up your business plan.

- Expect to use two business cards at each initial appointment. You will give one to the secretary when you arrive; she will keep that one for her file. When you are ushered in to meet the executive, you will give him or her another card.

Taiwan

Jan	1	Fr	Founding Day	May	1	Sa	Labor Day
Feb	15	Mo	Lunar New Year's Eve	Jun	18	Fr	Dragon Boat Festival
	16	Tu	Lunar New Year's Day	Sep	24	Fr	Mid-Autumn Festival
	17	We	Lunar New Year's holiday	Oct	10	Su	National Day
	18	Th	Lunar New Year's holiday	Nov	12	Fr	Birthday of Dr. Sun Yat Sen
Apr	5	Mo	Ching Ming Festival	Dec	25	Sa	Constitution Day

Standard time: Zone 20

- Modern Taiwan was founded by the Kuomintang forces who fled the mainland after being defeated by Mao Tse-tung's Communist forces in 1949. The relationship between Taiwan and the People's Republic of China remains tense. China views Taiwan as a renegade province which will eventually be reabsorbed into China. The PRC has also promised to invade if Taiwan ever declares itself an independent country.

- The linguistic reforms made by Communist China were never adopted in Taiwan. When you have your business card or promotional materials translated into Chinese for use in Taiwan, make sure that the translation is into pre-reform Chinese.

Thailand

Jan	1	Fr	New Year's Day	Jul	27	Tu	Aslahapuja Day
Mar	1	Mo	Macha Bucha Day		28	We	Khao Phansa Day
Apr	6	Su	Chakri Day	Aug	12	Th	H.M. the Queen's Birthday
	12	Mo	Songkran Festival (3 days)	Oct	23	Sa	Chulalongkorn Day
May	1	Sa	National Labor Day	Dec	5	Su	H.M. the King's Birthday
	5	We	Coronation Day		10	Fr	Constitution Day
	29	Sa	Visakha Bucha Day		31	Sa	New Year's Eve

Standard time: Zone 19

- Harmony is prized in Thailand. Voices are kept quiet, gestures are small, smiles are ubiquitous (although they do not necessarily indicate happiness), and confrontations are avoided whenever possible. Staring is considered rude, although Thais often stare at unfamiliar foreigners.

- Doing business in Bangkok is challenging; the city is noisy, hot, loud and choked with traffic. Give yourself plenty of time to get to your appointments.

- Traditional Thai customs (such as harmony and politeness) are often abandoned under the pressure of living in Bangkok. Outside the city, traditional Thai virtues are more common.

Turkey

Jan	1	Fr	New Year's Day	May	19	We	Youth and Sports Day
	18	Mo	Ramadan Feast (3 days)	Aug	30	Mo	Victory Day
Mar	23	Fr	National Sovereignty and Children's Day	Oct	29	Fr	Republic Day
	27	Sa	Kurban Bairam (4 days)				

Standard time: Zone 14

- Although most Turks are Muslim, Turkey is a secular country. The official language is Turkish (not Arabic). Since 1928, Turkish has been written in the Latin alphabet.

- Age is highly respected in Turkey. Elders are introduced first, served first, and are allowed to go through a doorway first. Children even kiss the right hand of elders to show respect. In a family-owned business, the decision-maker is probably an elder, even if some other member of the family does most of the negotiating.

- The term for a citizen of Turkey is *Turk*. *Turkmen* refers to someone from the Central Asian country of Turkmenistan (formerly part of the USSR).

- Times are changing in Turkey. There are now many Turkish women engaged in business. Younger people no longer follow all the traditional customs.

Ukraine

Jan	1	Fr	New Year's Day	May	9	Su	Victory Day
	7	Tu	Christmas Day		31	Mo	Trinity Monday
Mar	8	Mo	International Women's Day	Jun	28	Mo	Constitution Day
Apr	11	Su	Easter	Aug	24	Tu	Independence Day
May	1	Sa	Labor Day holiday	Nov	8	Mo	Revolution Day (2 days)
	2	Su	Labor Day holiday				

Standard time: Zone 15

- Ukrainians usually have three names, which are stated in this order: a given name, a patronymic, and a surname. A patronymic is derived from the given name of one's father; it means *"son of ___"* or *"daughter of ___."*

- Ukrainian women traditionally added the letter *"a"* on the end of their surnames. Although not all Ukrainians follow this practice today, it is not uncommon.

- While there are some surnames (such as those ending in *"-enko"*) which are characteristically Ukrainian, there has been so much inter-marriage between Russians and Ukrainians that this is no longer a reliable guide. Despite their surnames, a person named *Lysenko* could consider himself Russian, while a woman named *Ivanova* might consider herself Ukrainian.

United Kingdom

Jan	1	Fr	New Year's Day	May	31	Mo	Spring bank holiday[1]
	4	Mo	Bank holiday	Jul	12	Mo	Orangeman's Day[3]
Mar	17	We	St. Patrick's Day[3]	Aug	2	Mo	Bank holiday[2]
Apr	2	Fr	Good Friday		30	Mo	Summer bank holiday[1]
	5	Mo	Easter Monday[1]	Sep	20	Mo	Autumn holiday[2]
	6	Tu	Easter Tuesday[3]	Dec	25	Sa	Christmas Day
May	3	Mo	May Day		26	Su	Boxing Day
	17	Mo	Victoria Day[2]				

1. England and Wales
2. Scotland
3. Northern Ireland

Standard time: Zone 12

- The United Kingdom of Great Britain and Northern Ireland includes four distinct regions: England, Wales, Scotland and Northern Ireland. Most inhabitants of Wales, Scotland and Northern Ireland do not consider themselves English, and do not like being referred to as English.

- The term Great Britain refers to the island which encompasses England, Scotland and Wales. When referring to a person from Great Britain, the adjective *Briton* is generally preferred to *Britisher* or *Brit*.

United States

Jan	1	Fr	New Year's Day	Sep	6	Mo	Labor Day
	18	Mo	Martin Luther King, Jr. Day	Oct	11	Mo	Columbus Day
Feb	15	Mo	Washington's Birthday	Nov	11	Th	Veterans Day
May	31	Mo	Memorial Day		25	Th	Thanksgiving
Jul	4	Su	Independence Day	Dec	25	Sa	Christmas Day

Standard time: Zones 2, 3, 4, 5, 6, 7
    Aleutian Islands and Hawaii: Zone 2
    Alaska: Zone 3
    Pacific (San Francisco, Los Angeles): Zone 4
    Mountain (Denver): Zone 5
    Central (Chicago, Houston, Saint Louis): Zone 6
    Eastern (New York, Washington, D.C., Miami): Zone 7

- Business generally moves at a faster pace in the USA than in any other country in the world. Decisions are often made quickly. (This does not mean that payment is tendered quickly. There is anecdotal evidence that large US corporations are taking longer than ever to pay their bills.)

- During business discussions, silence tends to make US executives uncomfortable, and may prompt them to make a better offer.

- In addition, social relations are less important in the USA than elsewhere. In a recent survey, 72% of US executives said that they were willing to conduct business with someone they did not personally like.

- The USA is often a highly litigious society, and business decisions are also made in regard to legal liability.

Uruguay

Jan	1	Fr	New Year's Day	May	18	Tu	Battle of Las Piedras
	6	We	Children's Day (Epiphany)	Jun	19	Sa	Artigas Day
Feb	15	Mo	Carnival (2 days)	Jul	18	Su	Constitution Day
Apr	1	Th	Holy Thursday	Aug	25	We	Independence Day
	2	Fr	Good Friday	Oct	12	Tu	Columbus Day
	19	Mo	Landing of the 33 Orientals	Nov	1	Mo	All Saints Day
May	1	Sa	Labor Day	Dec	25	Sa	Christmas Day

Standard time: Zone 9

- Uruguay is the smallest of the Spanish-speaking countries of South America. It borders just two countries, Argentina and Brazil—the two largest nations in South America. In fact, Uruguay owes its existence to the fact that it serves as a buffer nation between these two aggressive giants.

- Ethnically, about 86.0% of Uruguayans are direct descendants of European immigrants. Immigrants to Uruguay came from all over Europe, but Spaniards and Italians predominate. Other substantial populations included Germans, English, Slavs, and Eastern European Jews.

- Uruguay has the highest per capita urban population in Latin America. About 87% of Uruguayans live in urban zones, the majority of them in or around the capital of Montevideo.

- Like the Argentines, the Uruguayans are big fans of the *tango*. *Tango* refers to a style of music, not just a dance, and many *tango* compositions are intended for listening, not dance. Uruguay also has an indigenous form of Afro-Uruguayan music and dance called the *candombe*.

- A common drink in Uruguay is *mate* (pronounced "mah-tay"). It is a drink prepared from the *yerba mate* leaf (*Ilex paraguayensis*), and is also known as *Paraguayan tea*. Uruguayans of every social and economic class drink it. It is not alcoholic, but, like coffee and tea, it contains caffeine. (See the note under Paraguay for instructions on drinking *mate*.)

Venezuela

Jan	1	Fr	New Year's Day	Jul	5	Mo	Firma Acta de Independencia
Feb	15	Mo	Carnival (2 days)		24	Sa	Simon Bolivar's Birthday
Apr	1	Th	Holy Thursday	Oct	12	Tu	Columbus Day
	2	Fr	Good Friday	Nov	1	Mo	All Saints Day
	19	Mo	Constitution Day	Dec	8	We	Immaculate Conception
May	1	Sa	International Labor Day		25	Sa	Christmas Day
Jun	24	Th	Battle of Carabobo				

Standard time: Zone 8

- Venezuela is blessed with many natural resources, having vast reserves of oil, coal, and bauxite. There is also great hydroelectric potential.

- Although many Venezuelans remain poor, decades of oil exports have created a sizable middle- and upper-class with a high standard of living. The recent drop in the price of petroleum now threatens many of Venezuela's economic gains.

- Venezuela is the most Caribbean of the South American Spanish-speaking nations, not only in geography but in attitude as well. Many Venezuelans display an easygoing enjoyment of life which is quite different from their South American neighbors.

- Venezuela's labor laws make it expensive to fire an employee or agent. Because of this, foreign firms often prefer to use commissioned agents rather than hired agents. (In most cases, a commissioned agent is not considered an employee.)

- Clothes make the man (and woman) in Venezuela. Dress is considered an important indicator of a person's status. Business attire should be conservative but stylish.

Vietnam

Jan	1	Fr	New Year's Day	May	1	Sa	Labor Day
	15	Fr	Lunar New Year (4 days)	Sep	2	Th	National Day
Apr	30	Fr	Liberation Day				

Standard time: Zone 8

- The official language is Vietnamese, although it is not spoken by all of Vietnam's many ethnic groups. Spoken Vietnamese is a tonal language and uses sounds not found in English, making it very difficult for Westerners to master. Written Vietnamese uses the Latin alphabet, with the addition of several diacritical marks. Foreigners often find it easier to communicate in written Vietnamese.

- Vietnamese name order is surname, followed by middle name, followed by given name (the opposite of English name order). Most Vietnamese have three names. Traditionally, the middle name indicated one's gender: all girls had the middle name *Thi*, and all boys had the middle name *Van*. But this tradition is no longer universal, and was never customary among Vietnam's other ethnic groups. Nowadays, the middle name is likely to be a second given name. People are addressed by an honorific and their given name (the last name of the three).

- Numerous honorifics are used in Vietnam. The most basic are *anh* (roughly equivalent to *Mister*) and *cô* (*Miss*). But there are many others, used for various ranks of people. The system is complex; *ông* (*Grandfather*) is used to address a respected older man, but *chú* (*Uncle*) is used to address a man who is older than you but younger than your father! To simplify matters, foreigners often resort to "Mister" and "Ms."

- The traditional Vietnamese greeting is a slight bow. Unlike the Japanese, the Vietnamese clasp their hands and hold them at waist level when they bow. Vietnamese who do business with Westerners are accustomed to adding a handshake as well. There is no casual contact between the genders in Vietnam, so Vietnamese men do not usually shake hands with women, or vice versa. The same bow is used upon departure.

- As in other Asian cultures, the Vietnamese consider it polite to avoid saying "No" whenever possible. Foreigners must learn to discern the difference between a true "Yes" and a "I'm saying 'Yes' to be polite but I really mean 'No.'" (One hint: "Maybe" always means "No.")

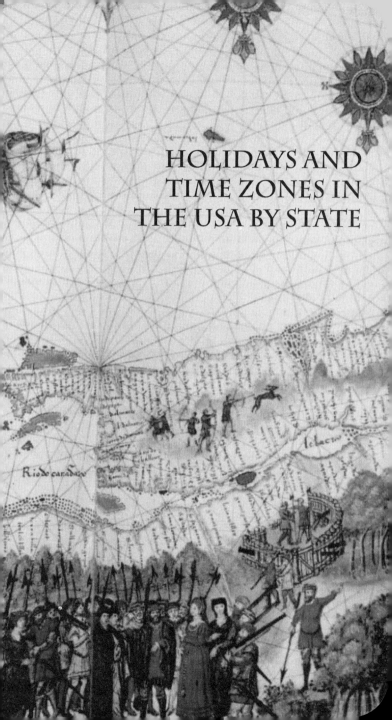

HOLIDAYS AND TIME ZONES IN THE USA BY STATE

INTRODUCTION

On the following pages are listed the 50 states and the District of Columbia in the United States of America and their holidays.

Time zone information for each state is shown below the list of holidays. For help in determining the time difference between two states, or between locations in the United States and another country, see the section on Time Difference Tables. All states except Arizona, Hawaii, and parts of Indiana observe daylight saving time. Be aware that daylight saving time may be in effect in the states concerned.

Alabama

Jan	1	Fr	New Year's Day	Jul	4	Su	Independence Day
	18	Mo	Robert E. Lee/Martin Luther King, Jr. Day	Sep	6	Mo	Labor Day
Feb	15	Mo	Presidents' Day	Oct	11	Mo	Columbus Day
	16	Tu	Mardi Gras Day (Baldwin, Mobile)	Nov	11	Th	Veterans Day
Apr	26	Mo	Confederate Memorial Day		25	Th	Thanksgiving
May	31	Mo	Memorial Day	Dec	25	Sa	Christmas Day
Jun	7	Mo	Jefferson Davis Day				

Standard time: Eastern, Zone 7

Alaska

Jan	1	Fr	New Year's Day	Sep	6	Mo	Labor Day
	18	Mo	Martin Luther King, Jr. Day	Oct	11	Mo	Columbus Day
Feb	15	Mo	Presidents' Day		18	Mo	Alaska Day
Mar	29	Mo	Sewards Day	Nov	11	Th	Veterans Day
May	31	Mo	Memorial Day		25	Th	Thanksgiving
Jul	4	Su	Independence Day	Dec	24	Fr	Christmas Eve
	5	Mo	Independence Day observed		25	Sa	Christmas Day

Standard time: Alaska, Zone 3; Aleutian Chain, Zone 2

Arizona

Jan	1	Fr	New Year's Day	Sep	6	Mo	Labor Day
	18	Mo	Martin Luther King, Jr. Day	Oct	11	Mo	Columbus Day
Feb	15	Mo	Presidents' Day	Nov	11	Th	Veterans Day
May	31	Mo	Memorial Day		25	Th	Thanksgiving
Jul	4	Su	Independence Day	Dec	25	Sa	Christmas Day

Standard time: Mountain, Zone 5

Arkansas

Jan	1	Fr	New Year's Day	Oct	11	Mo	Columbus Day
	18	Mo	Martin Luther King, Jr. Day	Nov	11	Th	Veterans Day
Feb	15	Mo	Presidents' Day		25	Th	Thanksgiving
May	31	Mo	Memorial Day	Dec	24	Fr	Christmas Eve
Jul	4	Su	Independence Day		25	Sa	Christmas Day
Sep	6	Mo	Labor Day				

Standard time: Central, Zone 6

California

Jan	1	Fr	New Year's Day	Oct	11	Mo	Columbus Day
	18	Mo	Martin Luther King, Jr. Day	Nov	11	Th	Veterans Day
Feb	12	Fr	Lincoln's Birthday		25	Th	Thanksgiving
	15	Mo	Washington's Birthday		26	Fr	Thanksgiving holiday
May	31	Mo	Memorial Day	Dec	24	Fr	Christmas Eve
Jul	5	Mo	Independence Day observed		25	Sa	Christmas Day
Sep	6	Mo	Labor Day				

Standard time: Pacific, Zone 4

Colorado

Jan	1	Fr	New Year's Day	Sep	6	Mo	Labor Day
	18	Mo	Martin Luther King, Jr. Day	Oct	11	Mo	Columbus Day
Feb	15	Mo	Presidents' Day	Nov	11	Th	Veterans Day
May	31	Mo	Memorial Day		25	Th	Thanksgiving
Jul	5	Mo	Independence Day observed	Dec	24	Fr	Christmas Day observed

Standard time: Mountain, Zone 5

Connecticut

Jan	1	Fr	New Year's Day	Jul	5	Mo	Independence Day
	18	Mo	Martin Luther King, Jr. Day	Sep	6	Mo	Labor Day
Feb	12	Fr	Lincoln's Birthday	Oct	11	Mo	Columbus Day
	15	Mo	Washington's Birthday	Nov	11	Th	Veterans Day
Apr	2	Fr	Good Friday		25	Th	Thanksgiving
May	31	Mo	Memorial Day	Dec	24	Fr	Christmas Day

Standard time: Eastern, Zone 7

Delaware

Jan	1	Fr	New Year's Day	Oct	11	Mo	Columbus Day
	18	Mo	Martin Luther King, Jr. Day	Nov	11	Th	Veterans Day
Feb	15	Mo	Presidents' Day		25	Th	Thanksgiving
Apr	2	Fr	Good Friday		26	Fr	Thanksgiving holiday
May	31	Mo	Memorial Day	Dec	24	Fr	Christmas Day
Jul	4	Su	Independence Day		31	Fr	New Year's Eve
Sep	6	Mo	Labor Day				

Standard time: Eastern, Zone 7

District of Columbia

Jan	1	Fr	New Year's Day	Sep	6	Mo	Labor Day
	18	Mo	Martin Luther King, Jr. Day	Oct	11	Mo	Columbus Day
Feb	15	Mo	Presidents' Day	Nov	11	Th	Veterans Day
May	31	Mo	Memorial Day		25	Th	Thanksgiving
Jul	4	Su	Independence Day	Dec	25	Sa	Christmas Day

Standard time: Eastern, Zone 7

Florida

Jan	1	Fr	New Year's Day	Sep	6	Mo	Labor Day
	18	Mo	Martin Luther King, Jr. Day	Oct	11	Mo	Columbus Day
Feb	12	Fr	Lincoln's Birthday	Nov	11	Th	Veterans Day
	15	Mo	Washington's Birthday		25	Th	Thanksgiving
May	31	Mo	Memorial Day		26	Fr	Thanksgiving holiday
Jul	4	Su	Independence Day	Dec	25	Sa	Christmas Day
	5	Mo	Independence Day observed				

Standard time:
> Central (Pensacola to Blountstown): Zone 6
> Eastern (Bristol to Miami): Zone 7

Georgia

Jan	1	Fr	New Year's Day		5	Mo	Independence Day observed
	18	Mo	Martin Luther King, Jr. Day	Sep	6	Mo	Labor Day
	19	Tu	Robert E. Lee's Birthday	Oct	11	Mo	Columbus Day
Feb	15	Mo	Presidents' Day	Nov	11	Th	Veterans Day
Apr	26	Mo	Confederate Memorial Day		25	Th	Thanksgiving
May	31	Mo	Memorial Day	Dec	24	Fr	Christmas Eve
Jul	4	Su	Independence Day		25	Sa	Christmas Day

Standard time: Eastern, Zone 7

Hawaii

Jan	1	Fr	New Year's Day	Aug	20	Fr	Admission Day
	18	Mo	Martin Luther King, Jr. Day	Sep	6	Mo	Labor Day
Feb	15	Mo	Presidents' Day	Nov	11	Th	Veterans Day
Mar	26	Fr	Prince Jonah Kuhio Kalanianaole Day		25	Th	Thanksgiving
Apr	2	Fr	Good Friday	Dec	24	Fr	Christmas Eve
May	31	Mo	Memorial Day		25	Sa	Christmas Day
Jun	11	Fr	King Kamehameha Day		31	Fr	New Year's Day 2000
Jul	5	Mo	Independence Day observed				

Standard time: Aleutian/Hawaii, Zone 2

Idaho

Jan	1	Fr	New Year's Day	Sep	6	Mo	Labor Day
	18	Mo	Martin Luther King, Jr. Day	Oct	11	Mo	Columbus Day
Feb	15	Mo	Presidents' Day	Nov	11	Th	Veterans Day
May	31	Mo	Memorial Day		25	Th	Thanksgiving
Jul	4	Su	Independence Day	Dec	24	Fr	Christmas Eve
	5	Mo	Independence Day observed		25	Sa	Christmas Day

Standard time:
Pacific (Lewiston): Zone 4
Mountain (Boise): Zone 5

Illinois

Jan	1	Fr	New Year's Day	Jul	5	Mo	Independence Day observed
	18	Mo	Martin Luther King, Jr. Day	Sep	6	Mo	Labor Day
Feb	12	Fr	Lincoln's Birthday	Oct	11	Mo	Columbus Day
	15	Mo	Washington's Birthday	Nov	11	Th	Veterans Day
Mar	1	Mo	Casimir Pulaski's Birthday		25	Th	Thanksgiving
Apr	2	Fr	Good Friday		26	Fr	Thanksgiving holiday
May	31	Mo	Memorial Day	Dec	24	Fr	Christmas Eve
Jul	4	Su	Independence Day		25	Sa	Christmas Day

Standard time: Central, Zone 6

Indiana

Jan	1	Fr	New Year's Day	Oct	11	Mo	Columbus Day
	18	Mo	Martin Luther King, Jr. Day	Nov	11	Th	Veterans Day
Apr	2	Fr	Good Friday		25	Th	Thanksgiving
May	31	Mo	Memorial Day		26	Fr	Thanksgiving holiday
Jul	4	Su	Independence Day	Dec	24	Fr	Christmas Eve
	5	Mo	Independence Day observed		25	Sa	Christmas Day
Sep	6	Mo	Labor Day				

Standard time:
  Central (Gary, Evansville), Zone 6
  Eastern (Indianapolis, South Bend), Zone 7

Iowa

Jan	1	Fr	New Year's Day	Jul	4	Su	Independence Day
	18	Mo	Martin Luther King, Jr. Day	Sep	6	Mo	Labor Day
Feb	12	Fr	Lincoln's Birthday	Nov	11	Th	Veterans Day
	15	Mo	Washington's Birthday		25	Th	Thanksgiving
May	31	Mo	Memorial Day	Dec	25	Sa	Christmas Day

Standard time: Central, Zone 6

Kansas

Jan	1	Fr	New Year's Day	Oct	11	Mo	Columbus Day
	18	Mo	Martin Luther King, Jr. Day	Nov	11	Th	Veterans Day
Feb	15	Mo	Presidents' Day		25	Th	Thanksgiving
May	31	Mo	Memorial Day		26	Fr	Thanksgiving holiday
Jul	4	Su	Independence Day	Dec	24	Fr	Christmas Eve
Sep	6	Mo	Labor Day		25	Sa	Christmas Day

Standard time:
  Mountain (Tribune): Zone 5
  Central (Witchita, Kansas City): Zone 6

Kentucky

Jan	1	Fr	New Year's Day	Sep	6	Mo	Labor Day
	18	Mo	Martin Luther King, Jr. Day	Nov	25	Th	Thanksgiving
Feb	15	Mo	Presidents' Day		26	Fr	Thanksgiving holiday
Apr	2	Fr	Good Friday	Dec	24	Fr	Christmas Eve
May	31	Mo	Memorial Day		25	Sa	Christmas Day
Jul	4	Su	Independence Day				

Standard time:
Central (Bowling Green): Zone 6
Eastern (Louisville): Zone 7

Louisiana

Jan	1	Fr	New Year's Day	Jul	5	Mo	Independence Day observed
	18	Mo	Martin Luther King, Jr. Day	Sep	6	Mo	Labor Day
Feb	15	Mo	Presidents' Day	Nov	11	Th	Veterans Day
	15	Tu	Mardi Gras		25	Th	Thanksgiving
Apr	2	Fr	Good Friday		26	Fr	Thanksgiving holiday
May	31	Mo	Memorial Day	Dec	24	Fr	Christmas Eve
Jul	4	Su	Independence Day		25	Sa	Christmas Day

Standard time: Central, Zone 6

Maine

Jan	1	Fr	New Year's Day	Sep	6	Mo	Labor Day
	18	Mo	Martin Luther King, Jr. Day	Oct	11	Mo	Columbus Day
Feb	15	Mo	Presidents' Day	Nov	11	Th	Veterans Day
Apr	19	Mo	Patriot's Day		25	Th	Thanksgiving
May	31	Mo	Memorial Day		26	Fr	Thanksgiving holiday
Jul	4	Su	Independence Day	Dec	24	Fr	Christmas Eve
	5	Mo	Independence Day observed		25	Sa	Christmas Day

Standard time: Eastern, Zone 7

Maryland

Jan	1	Fr	New Year's Day	Oct	11	Mo	Columbus Day
	18	Mo	Martin Luther King, Jr. Day	Nov	11	Th	Veterans Day
Feb	15	Mo	Presidents' Day		25	Th	Thanksgiving
May	31	Mo	Memorial Day		26	Fr	Thanksgiving holiday
Jul	5	Su	Independence Day	Dec	24	Fr	Christmas Day
Sep	6	Mo	Labor Day				

Standard time: Eastern, Zone 7

Massachusetts

Jan	1	Fr	New Year's Day	Jul	4	Su	Independence Day
	18	Mo	Martin Luther King, Jr. Day	Sep	6	Mo	Labor Day
Feb	15	Mo	Presidents' Day	Oct	11	Mo	Columbus Day
Mar	17	We	Evacuation Day	Nov	11	Th	Veterans Day
Apr	19	Mo	Patriots Day		25	Th	Thanksgiving
May	31	Mo	Memorial Day	Dec	25	Sa	Christmas Day
Jun	17	Th	Bunker Hill Day				

Standard time: Eastern, Zone 7

Michigan

Jan	1	Fr	New Year's Day	Sep	6	Mo	Labor Day
	18	Mo	Martin Luther King, Jr. Day	Oct	11	Mo	Columbus Day
Feb	15	Mo	Presidents' Day	Nov	11	Th	Veterans Day
May	31	Mo	Memorial Day		25	Th	Thanksgiving
Jul	4	Su	Independence Day	Dec	25	Sa	Christmas Day

Standard time:
Eastern: Zone 7
Central (Menominee, Dickenson, Iron, and Gogebic Counties): Zone 6

Minnesota

Jan	1	Fr	New Year's Day	Sep	6	Mo	Labor Day
	18	Mo	Martin Luther King, Jr. Day	Nov	11	Th	Veterans Day
Feb	15	Mo	Presidents' Day		25	Th	Thanksgiving
May	31	Mo	Memorial Day		26	Fr	Thanksgiving holiday
Jul	5	Su	Independence Day	Dec	24	Fr	Christmas Day

Standard time: Central: Zone 6

Mississippi

Jan	1	Fr	New Year's Day	Sep	6	Mo	Labor Day
	18	Mo	Martin Luther King, Jr. Day	Oct	11	Mo	Columbus Day
Feb	15	Mo	Presidents' Day	Nov	11	Th	Veterans Day
Apr	26	Mo	Confederate Memorial Day		25	Th	Thanksgiving
May	31	Mo	Memorial Day		26	Fr	Thanksgiving holiday
Jul	4	Su	Independence Day	Dec	24	Fr	Christmas Eve
	5	Mo	Independence Day observed		25	Sa	Christmas Day

Standard time: Central: Zone 6

Missouri

Jan	1	Fr	New Year's Day	Jul	5	Mo	Independence Day observed
	18	Mo	Martin Luther King, Jr. Day	Sep	6	Mo	Labor Day
Feb	12	Fr	Lincoln's Birthday	Oct	11	Mo	Columbus Day
	15	Mo	Washington's Birthday	Nov	11	Th	Veterans Day
May	8	Sa	Truman Day		25	Th	Thanksgiving
	31	Mo	Memorial Day	Dec	24	Fr	Christmas Eve
Jul	4	Su	Independence Day		25	Sa	Christmas Day

Standard time: Central: Zone 6

Montana

Jan	1	Fr	New Year's Day	Sep	6	Mo	Labor Day
	18	Mo	Martin Luther King, Jr. Day	Oct	11	Mo	Columbus Day
Feb	15	Mo	Presidents' Day	Nov	11	Th	Veterans Day
May	31	Mo	Memorial Day		25	Th	Thanksgiving
Jul	4	Su	Independence Day	Dec	24	Fr	Christmas Eve
	5	Mo	Independence Day observed		25	Sa	Christmas Day

Standard time: Mountain, Zone 5

Nebraska

Jan	1	Fr	New Year's Day	Sep	6	Mo	Labor Day
	18	Mo	Martin Luther King, Jr. Day	Oct	11	Mo	Columbus Day
Feb	15	Mo	Presidents' Day	Nov	11	Th	Veterans Day
Apr	30	Fr	Arbor Day		25	Th	Thanksgiving
May	31	Mo	Memorial Day		26	Fr	Thanksgiving holiday
Jul	4	Su	Independence Day	Dec	24	Fr	Christmas Eve
	5	Mo	Independence Day observed		25	Sa	Christmas Day

Standard time:
Mountain (Scottsbluff): Zone 5
Central (Lincoln): Zone 6

Nevada

Jan	1	Fr	New Year's Day	Oct	11	Mo	Columbus Day
	18	Mo	Martin Luther King, Jr. Day		31	Su	Nevada Day
Feb	15	Mo	Presidents' Day	Nov	1	Mo	Nevada Day observed
May	31	Mo	Memorial Day		11	Th	Veterans Day
Jul	4	Su	Independence Day		25	Th	Thanksgiving
	5	Mo	Independence Day observed		26	Fr	Family Day
Sep	6	Mo	Labor Day	Dec	25	Sa	Christmas Day

Standard time: Pacific, Zone 4

New Hampshire

Jan	1	Fr	New Year's Day	Oct	11	Mo	Columbus Day
	18	Mo	Civil Rights Day	Nov	11	Th	Veterans Day
Feb	15	Mo	Presidents' Day		25	Th	Thanksgiving
May	31	Mo	Memorial Day		26	Fr	Thanksgiving holiday
Jul	4	Su	Independence Day	Dec	24	Fr	Christmas Eve
	5	Mo	Independence Day observed		25	Sa	Christmas Day
Sep	6	Mo	Labor Day				

Standard time: Eastern, Zone 7

New Jersey

Jan	1	Fr	New Year's Day	Jul	5	Mo	Independence Day observed
	18	Mo	Martin Luther King, Jr. Day	Sep	6	Mo	Labor Day
Feb	12	Fr	Lincoln's Birthday	Oct	11	Mo	Columbus Day
	15	Mo	Washington's Birthday	Nov	11	Th	Veterans Day
Apr	2	Fr	Good Friday		25	Th	Thanksgiving
May	31	Mo	Memorial Day	Dec	24	Fr	Christmas Eve
Jul	4	Su	Independence Day		25	Sa	Christmas Day

Standard time: Eastern, Zone 7

New Mexico

Jan	1	Fr	New Year's Day	Oct	11	Mo	Columbus Day
	18	Mo	Martin Luther King, Jr. Day	Nov	11	Th	Veterans Day
Feb	15	Mo	Presidents' Day		25	Th	Thanksgiving
May	31	Mo	Memorial Day		26	Fr	Thanksgiving holiday
Jul	4	Su	Independence Day	Dec	24	Fr	Christmas Eve
	5	Mo	Independence Day observed		25	Sa	Christmas Day
Sep	6	Mo	Labor Day				

Standard time: Mountain, Zone 5

New York

Jan	1	Fr	New Year's Day	Sep	6	Mo	Labor Day
	18	Mo	Martin Luther King, Jr. Day	Oct	11	Mo	Columbus Day
Feb	12	Fr	Lincoln's Birthday	Nov	11	Th	Veterans Day
	15	Mo	Washington's Birthday		25	Th	Thanksgiving
May	31	Mo	Memorial Day	Dec	25	Sa	Christmas Day
Jul	4	Su	Independence Day				

Standard time: Eastern, Zone 7

North Carolina

Jan	1	Fr	New Year's Day	Sep	6	Mo	Labor Day
	18	Mo	Martin Luther King, Jr. Day	Oct	11	Mo	Columbus Day
Feb	15	Mo	Presidents' Day	Nov	11	Th	Veterans Day
Apr	2	Fr	Good Friday		25	Th	Thanksgiving
May	31	Mo	Memorial Day		26	Fr	Thanksgiving holiday
Jul	4	Su	Independence Day	Dec	25	Sa	Christmas Day

Standard time: Eastern, Zone 7

North Dakota

Jan	1	Fr	New Year's Day	Oct	11	Mo	Columbus Day
	18	Mo	Martin Luther King, Jr. Day	Nov	11	Th	Veterans Day
Feb	15	Mo	Presidents' Day		25	Th	Thanksgiving
Apr	2	Fr	Good Friday		26	Fr	Thanksgiving holiday
May	31	Mo	Memorial Day	Dec	24	Fr	Christmas Eve
Jul	4	Su	Independence Day		25	Sa	Christmas Day
Sep	6	Mo	Labor Day		26	Su	Christmas holiday

Standard time:
Mountain, Zone 5
Central (Fargo): Zone 6

Ohio

Jan	1	Fr	New Year's Day	Oct	11	Mo	Columbus Day
	18	Mo	Martin Luther King, Jr. Day	Nov	11	Th	Veterans Day
Feb	15	Mo	Presidents' Day		25	Th	Thanksgiving
May	31	Mo	Memorial Day		26	Fr	Thanksgiving holiday
Jul	4	Su	Independence Day	Dec	24	Fr	Christmas Eve
	5	Mo	Independence Day observed		25	Sa	Christmas Day
Sep	6	Mo	Labor Day				

Standard time: Eastern, Zone 7

Oklahoma

Jan	1	Fr	New Year's Day	Oct	11	Mo	Columbus Day
	18	Mo	Martin Luther King, Jr. Day	Nov	11	Th	Veterans Day
Feb	15	Mo	Presidents' Day		25	Th	Thanksgiving
May	31	Mo	Memorial Day		26	Fr	Thanksgiving holiday
Jul	4	Su	Independence Day	Dec	24	Fr	Christmas Eve
	5	Mo	Independence Day observed		25	Sa	Christmas Day
Sep	6	Mo	Labor Day				

Standard time: Central, Zone 6

Oregon

Jan	1	Fr	New Year's Day	Sep	6	Mo	Labor Day
	18	Mo	Martin Luther King, Jr. Day	Oct	11	Mo	Columbus Day
Feb	15	Mo	Presidents' Day	Nov	11	Th	Veterans Day
May	31	Mo	Memorial Day		25	Th	Thanksgiving
Jul	4	Su	Independence Day	Dec	24	Fr	Christmas Eve
	5	Mo	Independence Day observed		25	Sa	Christmas Day

Standard time: Pacific, Zone 4

Pennsylvania

Jan	1	Fr	New Year's Day	Jul	5	Mo	Independence Day observed
	18	Mo	Martin Luther King, Jr. Day	Sep	6	Mo	Labor Day
Feb	12	Fr	Lincoln's Birthday	Oct	11	Mo	Columbus Day
	15	Mo	Presidents' Day	Nov	11	Th	Veterans Day
Apr	2	Fr	Good Friday		25	Th	Thanksgiving
May	31	Mo	Memorial Day		26	Fr	Thanksgiving holiday
Jun	14	Mo	Flag Day	Dec	24	Fr	Christmas Eve
Jul	4	Su	Independence Day		25	Sa	Christmas Day

Standard time: Eastern, Zone 7

Rhode Island

Jan	1	Fr	New Year's Day	Sep	6	Mo	Labor Day
	18	Mo	Martin Luther King, Jr. Day	Oct	11	Mo	Columbus Day
Feb	15	Mo	Presidents' Day	Nov	11	Th	Veterans Day
May	31	Mo	Memorial Day		25	Th	Thanksgiving
Jul	4	Su	Independence Day	Dec	24	Fr	Christmas Eve
Aug	9	Mo	Victory Day		25	Sa	Christmas Day

Standard time: Eastern, Zone 7

South Carolina

Jan	1	Fr	New Year's Day	Oct	11	Mo	Columbus Day
	18	Mo	Martin Luther King, Jr. Day	Nov	11	Th	Veterans Day
Feb	15	Mo	Presidents' Day		25	Th	Thanksgiving
May	31	Mo	Memorial Day		26	Fr	Thanksgiving holiday
Jul	4	Su	Independence Day	Dec	24	Fr	Christmas Eve
	5	Fr	Independence Day observed		25	Sa	Christmas Day
Sep	6	Mo	Labor Day		27	Mo	Christmas holiday

Standard time: Eastern, Zone 7

South Dakota

Jan	1	Fr	New Year's Day	Sep	6	Mo	Labor Day
	18	Mo	Martin Luther King, Jr. Day	Oct	11	Mo	Native Americans' Day
Feb	15	Mo	Presidents' Day	Nov	11	Th	Veterans Day
May	31	Mo	Memorial Day		25	Th	Thanksgiving
Jul	4	Su	Independence Day	Dec	24	Fr	Christmas Eve
	5	Mo	Independence Day observed		25	Sa	Christmas Day

Standard time:
Mountain (Rapid City): Zone 5
Central (Pierre, Sioux Falls): Zone 6

Tennessee

Jan	1	Fr	New Year's Day	Sep	6	Mo	Labor Day
	18	Mo	Martin Luther King, Jr. Day	Oct	11	Mo	Columbus Day
Feb	15	Mo	Presidents' Day	Nov	11	Th	Veterans Day
Apr	2	Fr	Good Friday		25	Th	Thanksgiving
May	31	Mo	Memorial Day	Dec	24	Fr	Christmas Eve
Jul	4	Su	Independence Day		25	Sa	Christmas Day
	5	Mo	Independence Day observed				

Standard time:
Central (Memphis, Nashville): Zone 6
Eastern (Chattanooga): Zone 7

Texas

Jan	1	Fr	New Year's Day	Jul	4	Su	Independence Day
	18	Mo	Martin Luther King, Jr. Day	Aug	27	Fr	Lyndon Baines Johnson Day
	19	Tu	Confederate Heroes Day	Sep	6	Mo	Labor Day
Feb	15	Mo	Presidents' Day	Nov	11	Th	Veterans Day
Mar	2	Tu	Texas Independence Day		25	Th	Thanksgiving
Apr	21	We	San Jacinto Day		26	Fr	Thanksgiving holiday
May	31	Mo	Memorial Day	Dec	24	Fr	Christmas Eve
Jun	19	Sa	Emancipation Day		25	Sa	Christmas Day

Standard time:
    Central (Memphis, Nashville): Zone 6
    Eastern (Chattanooga): Zone 7

Utah

Jan	1	Fr	New Year's Day	Sep	6	Mo	Labor Day
	18	Mo	Martin Luther King, Jr. Day	Oct	11	Mo	Columbus Day
Feb	15	Mo	Presidents' Day	Nov	11	Th	Veterans Day
May	31	Mo	Memorial Day		25	Th	Thanksgiving
Jul	4	Su	Independence Day	Dec	24	Fr	Christmas Eve
	5	Mo	Independence Day observed		25	Sa	Christmas Day
	24	Sa	Pioneer Day				

Standard time: Mountain, Zone 5

Vermont

Jan	1	Fr	New Year's Day	Sep	6	Mo	Labor Day
	18	Mo	Martin Luther King, Jr. Day	Oct	11	Mo	Columbus Day
Feb	15	Mo	Presidents' Day	Nov	11	Th	Veterans Day
Mar	2	Tu	Town Meeting Day		25	Th	Thanksgiving
May	31	Mo	Memorial Day		26	Fr	Thanksgiving holiday
Jul	4	Su	Independence Day	Dec	25	Sa	Christmas Day
Aug	16	Mo	Bennington Battle Day				

Standard time: Eastern, Zone 7

Virginia

Jan	1	Fr	New Year's Day	Oct	11	Mo	Columbus Day and York Town Victory Day
	18	Mo	Lee/Jackson/King Day	Nov	11	Th	Veterans Day
Feb	15	Mo	Presidents' Day		25	Th	Thanksgiving
May	31	Mo	Memorial Day		26	Fr	Thanksgiving holiday
Jul	4	Su	Independence Day	Dec	24	Fr	Christmas Eve
	5	Mo	Independence Day observed		25	Sa	Christmas Day
Sep	6	Mo	Labor Day				

Standard time: Eastern, Zone 7

Washington

Jan	1	Fr	New Year's Day	Sep	6	Mo	Labor Day
	18	Mo	Martin Luther King, Jr. Day	Oct	11	Mo	Columbus Day
Feb	12	Fr	Lincoln's Birthday	Nov	11	Th	Veterans Day
	15	Mo	Washington's Birthday		25	Th	Thanksgiving
May	31	Mo	Memorial Day		26	Fr	Thanksgiving holiday
Jul	4	Su	Independence Day	Dec	25	Sa	Christmas Day

Standard time: Pacific, Zone 4

Wisconsin

Jan	1	Fr	New Year's Day	Sep	6	Mo	Labor Day
	18	Mo	Martin Luther King, Jr. Day	Nov	25	Th	Thanksgiving
Feb	15	Mo	Presidents' Day	Dec	24	Fr	Christmas Eve
Apr	2	Fr	Good Friday		25	Sa	Christmas Day
May	31	Mo	Memorial Day		31	Fr	New Year's Eve
Jul	4	Su	Independence Day				

Standard time: Central, Zone 6

West Virginia

Jan	1	Fr	New Year's Day	Sep	6	Mo	Labor Day
	18	Mo	Martin Luther King, Jr. Day	Oct	11	Mo	Columbus Day
Feb	12	Fr	Lincoln's Birthday	Nov	11	Th	Veterans Day
	15	Mo	Washington's Birthday		25	Th	Thanksgiving
May	31	Mo	Memorial Day	Dec	24	Fr	Christmas Eve
Jun	20	Su	West Virginia Day		25	Sa	Christmas Day
Jul	4	Su	Independence Day		31	Fr	New Year's Eve

Standard time: Pacific, Zone 4

Wyoming

Jan	1	Fr	New Year's Day	Oct	11	Mo	Columbus Day
	18	Mo	Martin Luther King, Jr. Day/Equality Day	Nov	11	Th	Veterans Day
Feb	15	Mo	Presidents' Day		25	Th	Thanksgiving
May	31	Mo	Memorial Day		26	Fr	Thanksgiving holiday
Jul	4	Su	Independence Day	Dec	24	Fr	Christmas Eve
	5	Mo	Independence Day observed		25	Sa	Christmas Day
Sep	6	Mo	Labor Day				

Standard time: Mountain, Zone 5

HOLIDAYS BY DATE

INTRODUCTION

Holidays by date of 77 countries and US states are listed on the following pages. Because Sunday is a weekly holiday in most countries, the Sunday listings contain only places in which Sunday is not normally a holiday, such as Egypt, Israel, Kuwait, parts of Malaysia, Nepal, Pakistan, and Saudi Arabia.

Individual states observing holidays are listed under "United States," followed by that state's abbreviation. A list of state abbreviations appears below.

Alabama	AL	Montana	MT
Alaska	AK	Nebraska	NE
Arizona	AZ	Nevada	NV
Arkansas	AR	New Hampshire	NH
California	CA	New Jersey	NJ
Colorado	CO	New Mexico	NM
Connecticut	CT	New York	NY
Delaware	DE	North Carolina	NC
District of Columbia	DC	North Dakota	ND
Florida	FL	Ohio	OH
Georgia	GA	Oklahoma	OK
Hawaii	HI	Oregon	OR
Idaho	ID	Pennsylvania	PA
Illinois	IL	Rhode Island	RI
Indiana	IN	South Carolina	SC
Iowa	IA	South Dakota	SD
Kansas	KS	Tennessee	TN
Kentucky	KY	Texas	TX
Louisiana	LA	Utah	UT
Maine	ME	Vermont	VT
Maryland	MD	Virginia	VA
Massachusetts	MA	Washington	WA
Michigan	MI	West Virginia	WV
Minnesota	MN	Wisconsin	WI
Mississippi	MS	Wyoming	WY
Missouri	MO		

January

1   Fr

All listed countries
  except
Egypt
Israel
Malaysia
Nepal
Pakistan
Saudi Arabia
Sri Lanka

2   Sa

Japan
Kazakstan
Korea
Romania
Switzerland

3   Su

Japan

4   Mo

Canada
New Zealand
U.K.

6   We

Austria
Dominican Rep.
Finland
Germany
Greece
Italy
Puerto Rico
Slovak Rep.
Spain
Sweden
Switzerland
Uruguay

7   Th

Egypt
Russia
Ukraine

9   Sa

Panama

11   Mo

Colombia
Morocco
Nepal

12   Tu

Saudi Arabia

13   We

Puerto Rico
Saudi Arabia

14   Th

Saudi Arabia

15   Fr

Japan
Saudi Arabia
Sri Lanka
Vietnam

16   Sa

Saudi Arabia
Vietnam

17   Su

Saudi Arabia
Vietnam

18   Mo

Egypt
Kuwait
New Zealand
Puerto Rico
Saudi Arabia
Turkey
United States
Vietnam

19   Tu

Azerbaijan
Egypt
Kuwait
India
Indonesia
Malaysia
Morocco
Nigeria
Pakistan
Saudi Arabia
Singapore

Sri Lanka
Turkey
United States
  (GA, TX)

20   We

Azerbaijan
Egypt
Indonesia
Kuwait
Malaysia
Nigeria
Pakistan
Saudi Arabia
Turkey

21   Th

Dominican Rep.
Pakistan
Saudi Arabia

22   Fr

Nepal
Saudi Arabia

25   Mo

New Zealand

26   Tu

Australia
Dominican Rep.
India

30   Sa

Nepal

31   Su

Sri Lanka

February

1   Mo

Israel
New Zealand

4   Th

Sri Lanka

5 Fr

Mexico

6 Sa

New Zealand

9 Tu

Australia

11 Th

Japan

12 Fr

United States (CA,
CT, FL, IA, IL,
MO, NJ, NY, PA,
WA, WV)

14 Su

Korea
Nepal
Sri Lanka

15 Mo

Bolivia
Brazil
Canada
Korea
Panama
Puerto Rico
Taiwan
Uruguay
United States (all
except IN)
Venezuela

16 Tu

Bolivia
Brazil
China
Korea
Malaysia
Panama
Portugal
Singapore
Taiwan
United States (AL)
Uruguay
Venezuela

17 We

Brazil
China
Colombia
Jamaica
Korea
Malaysia
Panama
Singapore
Switzerland
Taiwan

18 Th

Taiwan

19 Fr

Canada
Nepal

22 Mo

Greece

24 We

Cuba

25 Th

Kuwait

26 Fr

Kuwait

27 Sa

Dominican Rep.

March

1 Mo

Australia
Korea
Nepal
Paraguay
Sri Lanka
Thailand
United States (IL)

2 Tu

China

Israel
United States
(TX, VT)

3 We

Morocco

8 Mo

Azerbaijan
China
Kazakstan
Nepal
New Zealand
Russia
Ukraine

9 Tu

Belize

12 Fr

Fiji

15 Mo

Australia
Hungary

17 We

Ireland
Nepal
U.K.
United States (MA)

18 Th

Indonesia

19 Fr

Costa Rica
Spain

20 Sa

Azerbaijan

21 Su

Azerbaijan
Japan
Mexico
South Africa

22 Mo

Colombia
Japan
Kazakstan
New Zealand
Puerto Rico
Saudi Arabia
South Africa

23 Tu

Pakistan
Saudi Arabia
Turkey

24 We

Saudi Arabia

25 Th

Greece
Nepal
Saudi Arabia

26 Fr

Nepal
Saudi Arabia
United States (HI)

27 Sa

Egypt
Saudi Arabia
Turkey

28 Su

Egypt
Indonesia
Kuwait
Malaysia
Nigeria
Norway
Pakistan
Saudi Arabia
Singapore
Switzerland
Turkey

29 Mo

Egypt
Kuwait
Nigeria
Pakistan
Saudi Arabia
Sri Lanka

Turkey
United States (AK)

30 Tu

Egypt
Kuwait
Pakistan
Saudi Arabia
Turkey

31 We

Egypt
El Salvador
Guatemala
Saudi Arabia
Sri Lanka

April

1 Th

Argentina
Brazil
Colombia
Costa Rica
Denmark
El Salvador
Guatemala
Honduras
Iceland
Israel
Mexico
Nicaragua
Norway
Panama
Paraguay
Peru
Philippines
Saudi Arabia
Spain
Uruguay
Venezuela

2 Fr

Argentina
Australia
Belize
Bolivia
Brazil
Canada
Chile
Colombia
Costa Rica
Denmark
Dominican Rep.

Ecuador
El Salvador
Fiji
Finland
Germany
Guatemala
Honduras
Iceland
Indonesia
Ireland
Israel
Jamaica
Mexico
Netherlands
New Zealand
Nicaragua
Nigeria
Norway
Panama
Paraguay
Peru
Philippines
Portugal
Puerto Rico
Saudi Arabia
Singapore
Slovak Rep.
South Africa
Spain
Sweden
Switzerland
U.K.
United States (CT,
   DE, HI, IL, IN, KY,
   LA, NJ, NC, ND,
   PA, TN, WI)
Uruguay
Venezuela

3 Sa

Belize
Brazil
Chile
Colombia
Fiji
Guatemala
Israel
Panama
Spain

4 Su

Belgium
Denmark
Finland
Germany
Israel
Italy

Norway
Senegal
Sweden
Switzerland

5   Mo

Australia
Austria
Belgium
Belize
Canada
Czech Rep.
Denmark
Fiji
Finland
France
Germany
Hungary
Iceland
Ireland
Israel
Italy
Jamaica
Korea
Madagascar
Netherlands
New Zealand
Nigeria
Norway
Poland
Senegal
Slovak Rep.
South Africa
Spain
Sweden
Switzerland
Taiwan
U.K.

6   Tu

Australia
Israel
Thailand
U.K.

7   We

Israel

8   Th

Azerbaijan
Pakistan

9   Fr

Greece

Pakistan
Philippines

11   Su

Costa Rica
Egypt
Romania
Ukraine

12   Mo

Egypt
Greece
Romania
Thailand

13   Tu

Egypt
Israel

14   We

Honduras
Nepal

17   Sa

Egypt
Indonesia
Kuwait
Malaysia

18   Su

Morocco

19   Mo

Cuba
United States (MA, ME)
Uruguay
Venezuela

20   Tu

Israel

21   We

Israel
Puerto Rico
United States (TX)

22   Th

Iceland

25   Su

Australia
Egypt
Italy
New Zealand
Portugal

26   Mo

Australia
United States (AL, GA, MS)

27   Tu

Morocco
South Africa

28   We

Morocco

29   Th

Japan

30   Fr

Finland
Netherlands
United States (NE)
Vietnam

May

1   Sa

Argentina
Austria
Belgium
Belize
Bolivia
Brazil
Chile
China
Colombia
Costa Rica
Cuba
Czech Rep.
Denmark
Dominican Rep.
Ecuador
Egypt
El Salvador
Finland
France
Germany

Greece
Guatemala
Honduras
Hungary
Iceland
India
Italy
Kazakstan
Madagascar
Malaysia
Mexico
Morocco
Nepal
Nicaragua
Nigeria
Norway
Pakistan
Panama
Paraguay
Peru
Philippines
Poland
Portugal
Romania
Russia
Senegal
Singapore
Slovak Rep.
South Africa
Spain
Sweden
Switzerland
Taiwan
Thailand
Ukraine
Uruguay
Venezuela
Vietnam

2 Su

Russia
Ukraine

3 Mo

Australia
Ireland
Japan
Poland
U.K.

4 Tu

China
Israel
Japan

5 We

Japan
Korea
Mexico
Netherlands
Thailand

8 Sa

Czech Rep.
France
Nepal
Slovak Rep.
United States
(MO)

9 Su

Kazakstan
Russia
Ukraine

13 Th

Austria
Belgium
Denmark
Finland
France
Germany
Iceland
Indonesia
Madagascar
Netherlands
Norway
Senegal
Sweden
Switzerland

14 Fr

Israel

15 Sa

Pakistan

17 Mo

Australia
Colombia
Nepal
Norway
U.K.

18 Tu

Uruguay

19 We

Turkey

21 Fr

Chile
Israel

22 Sa

Korea

23 Su

Belgium
Denmark
Finland
Germany
Morocco
Norway
Sweden
Switzerland

24 Mo

Belgium
Belize
Canada
Denmark
France
Germany
Hungary
Iceland
Jamaica
Madagascar
Norway
Senegal
Sweden
Switzerland

25 Tu

Argentina
Madagascar
Nepal

26 We

Nepal

28 Fr

Azerbaijan

29 Sa

Malaysia
Singapore
Thailand

30 Su

Indonesia
Nicaragua

31 Mo

Fiji
Greece
Netherlands
Puerto Rico
Ukraine
U.K.
United States

June

1 Tu

China
Dominican Rep.

3 Th

Austria
Bolivia
Brazil
Germany
Poland
Portugal
Switzerland

5 Sa

Denmark
Malaysia

6 Su

Korea

7 Mo

Australia
Colombia
Ireland
New Zealand
United States (AL)

10 Th

Portugal

11 Fr

United States (HI)

12 Sa

Fiji
Paraguay
Philippines
Russia

13 Su

Portugal

14 Mo

Argentina
Australia
Colombia
United States (PA)

15 Tu

Azerbaijan

16 We

South Africa

17 Th

Iceland
United States (MA)

18 Fr

China
Taiwan

19 Sa

United States (TX)
Uruguay

20 Su

Argentina
United States
(WV)

21 Mo

Argentina

23 We

Egypt

24 Th

Canada
Venezuela

25 Fr

Finland

26 Sa

Egypt
Indonesia
Kuwait
Madagascar
Malaysia
Morocco
Nigeria
Sweden

28 Mo

Fiji
Ukraine

29 Tu

Chile
Costa Rica
Italy
Peru

30 We

Guatemala

July

1 Th

Canada
China

4 Su

Puerto Rico
United States

5 Mo

Colombia
Czech Rep.
Slovak Rep.
Venezuela
United States (all
but AL, AR, AZ,
DC, DE, IA, KS,
KY, MA, MI, NC,
ND, NY, RI, TX,
VT, WA, WI, WV)

6 Tu
Czech Rep.

9 Fr
Argentina
Morocco

12 Mo
U.K.

14 We
France

17 Sa
Korea

18 Su
Uruguay

19 Mo
Nicaragua

20 Tu
Colombia
Japan

21 We
Belgium
Puerto Rico

22 Th
Israel

24 Sa
United States (UT)
Venezuela

25 Su
Costa Rica
Cuba
Puerto Rico
Spain

26 Mo
Fiji

27 Tu
Thailand

28 We
Peru
Puerto Rico
Thailand

29 Th
Peru

August

1 Su
China
Jamaica
Nicaragua
Switzerland

2 Mo
Australia
Canada
Costa Rica
Iceland
Ireland
U.K.

4 We
El Salvador

5 Th
El Salvador

6 Fr
Bolivia
El Salvador
Jamaica

7 Sa
Colombia

9 Mo
Singapore
South Africa
United States (RI)

10 Tu
Ecuador

12 Th
Thailand

14 Sa
Morocco
Pakistan

15 Su
Austria
Belgium
Chile
Costa Rica
France
Germany
Greece
Guatemala
India
Italy
Korea
Madagascar
Panama
Paraguay
Poland
Portugal
Senegal
Spain
Switzerland

16 Mo
Argentina
Colombia
Dominican Rep.
United States (VT)

17 Tu
Argentina
Indonesia

20 Fr
Canada
Hungary
Morocco
United States (HI)

22 Su
Russia

24 Tu

Ukraine

25 We

Uruguay

27 Fr

United States (TX)

29 Su

Philippines
Slovak Rep.

30 Mo

Kazakstan
Peru
Turkey
U.K.

31 Tu

Malaysia

September

1 We

Slovak Rep.

2 Th

Vietnam

5 Su

Nepal

6 Mo

Canada
Pakistan
Puerto Rico
United States

10 Fr

Belize

11 Sa

Israel
Pakistan
Spain

12 Su

Israel

14 Tu

Nicaragua

15 We

Costa Rica
El Salvador
Guatemala
Honduras
Japan
Korea
Nicaragua
Slovak Rep.

16 Th

Mexico

18 Sa

Chile

19 Su

Chile
Italy

20 Mo

Israel
Switzerland
U.K.

21 Tu

Belize

23 Th

Japan
Saudi Arabia

24 Fr

China
Dominican Rep.
Korea
South Africa
Taiwan

25 Sa

Korea

26 Su

Israel
Korea

27 Mo

Australia
New Zealand

29 We

India
Paraguay

30 Th

India

October

1 Fr

China
Israel
Nigeria

2 Sa

China
India
Israel

3 Su

Germany
Honduras

4 Mo

Australia

5 Tu

Portugal

6 We

Egypt

8 Fr

Peru

9 Sa

Azerbaijan
Ecuador

10 Su

Cuba
Japan
Taiwan

11 Mo

Argentina
Canada
Fiji
Japan
Puerto Rico
United States (all
  but HI, IA, KY, LA,
  MN, TX, WI)

12 Tu

Argentina
Belize
Brazil
Chile
Costa Rica
Dominican Rep.
Guatemala
Honduras
Mexico
Spain
Uruguay
Venezuela

18 Mo

Azerbaijan
Colombia
Jamaica
United States (AK)

20 We

Guatemala

21 Th

Honduras

22 Fr

New Zealand

23 Sa

Egypt
Hungary
Thailand

24 Su

Egypt

25 Mo

Ireland
Kazakstan
New Zealand

26 Tu

Austria

28 Th

Czech Rep.
Greece

29 Fr

Turkey

31 Su

Germany
United States (NV)

November

1 Mo

Austria
Belgium
Bolivia
Brazil
Chile
Colombia
France
Germany
Guatemala
Italy
Madagascar
New Zealand
Peru
Philippines
Poland
Portugal
Senegal
Slovak Rep.
Spain
Switzerland
Uruguay
Venezuela

2 Tu

Brazil
Ecuador
El Salvador
Mexico
Nicaragua

3 We

Ecuador
Japan
Panama

4 Th

Panama

5 Fr

Kuwait

6 Sa

Finland
Indonesia
Morocco
Sweden

7 Su

India
Malaysia
Russia
Singapore

8 Mo

Fiji
Singapore
Ukraine

9 Tu

Nepal

10 We

Panama

11 Th

Belgium
Canada
France
Poland
Puerto Rico
United States (all
  but KY, WI)

12 Fr

Azerbaijan
New Zealand
Taiwan

15 Mo

Brazil
Colombia

17 We

Azerbaijan
Germany

18 Th

Morocco

19 Fr

Belize
Puerto Rico

20 Sa

Mexico

23 Tu

Japan

25 Th

Puerto Rico
United States

26 Fr

United States (all
but AL, AK, AR,
AZ, CT, CO, DC,
HI, IA, ID, MA,
MI, MO, MT, NJ,
NY, OR, RI, SD,
TN, UT, WV, WI)

28 Su

Panama

29 Mo

New Zealand

30 Tu

Philippines

December

1 We

Austria
Portugal
Romania

3 Fr

Korea

4 Sa

Israel

5 Su

Thailand

6 Mo

Finland
Spain

7 Tu

Italy

8 We

Argentina
Austria
Brazil
Chile
Colombia
Italy
Nicaragua
Panama
Paraguay
Peru
Portugal
Spain
Switzerland
Venezuela

10 Fr

Kuwait
Thailand

11 Sa

Israel

12 Su

Mexico
Russia

16 Th

Kazakstan
South Africa

23 Th

Egypt
Japan

24 Fr

Brazil
Czech Rep.
Denmark
El Salvador
Finland
Guatemala
Iceland
Mexico
Panama
Portugal
Slovak Rep.
Sweden
Switzerland
United States (all
but AL, AZ, DC,
FL, IA, MA, MI,
NV, NC, NY, VT,
WA)

25 Sa

Argentina
Australia
Austria
Belgium
Belize
Bolivia
Brazil
Chile
Colombia
Costa Rica
Cuba
Czech Rep.
Denmark
Dominican Rep.
Ecuador
El Salvador
Fiji
Finland
France
Germany
Greece
Guatemala
Honduras
Hungary
Iceland
India
Indonesia

Ireland
Italy
Jamaica
Korea
Madagascar
Malaysia
Mexico
Netherlands
New Zealand
Nicaragua
Nigeria
Norway
Pakistan
Panama
Paraguay
Peru
Philippines
Poland
Portugal
Puerto Rico
Romania
Senegal
Singapore
Slovak Rep.
South Africa
Spain
Sweden
Switzerland
Taiwan
U.K.
United States
Uruguay
Venezuela

26 Su

Australia
Austria

Belize
Czech Rep.
Denmark
Finland
Germany
Greece
Hungary
Iceland
Ireland
Italy
Jamaica
Netherlands
Nigeria
Norway
Poland
Romania
Slovak Rep.
South Africa
Spain
Sweden
Switzerland
U.K.
United States (ND, SC)

27 Mo

Australia
Canada
Fiji
New Zealand
South Africa

28 Tu

Australia
Canada
New Zealand

29 We

Costa Rica
Nepal

30 Th

Costa Rica
Philippines

31 Fr

Argentina
Azerbaijan
Brazil
Costa Rica
El Salvador
Guatemala
Iceland
Japan
Mexico
Pakistan
Panama
Philippines
Sweden
Switzerland
Thailand
United States (DE, HI, WV, WI)

TIME DIFFERENCE TABLES

INTRODUCTION

The tables on the following pages will help you determine the time difference between two locations as well as the overlap in normal business hours.

- To calculate the time difference between two places, determine the time zone number for each place in the holiday list by country or state. Subtract the smaller number from the larger one. Time in the larger zone number is always later than in the place with the smaller zone number.

- After determining the difference in hours, examine the time difference table for that number. The time in the left column applies to the place with the smaller zone number. The time in the right column applies to the place with the larger zone number. Normal business hours for each place are in boldface type.

- As an example, to determine the overlap in business hours in New York and Frankfurt: New York's time zone number is 7; Frankfurt's time zone number is 13. Subtract 7 from 13; this gives us a value of 6. There is a 6 hour time difference; Frankfurt's time is 6 hours later than New York's. Examining the six-hour time difference table, we see there is a two-hour overlap in business hours. The time period from 9:00 AM to 11:00 AM in New York (smaller zone number) overlaps the time period from 3:00 PM to 5:00 PM in Frankfurt (larger zone number).

- Some countries use half-hour time zones. Determining a time difference might produce such a result such as 6½. When examining the tables in these cases, use the next-lower time difference table—i.e., for 6½, use 6—and add a half hour to the time in the "Larger zone number" column.

1 hour difference		**2** hour difference		**3** hour difference	
Smaller zone number	Larger zone number	Smaller zone number	Larger zone number	Smaller zone number	Larger zone number
1 AM	2 AM	1 AM	3 AM	1 AM	4 AM
2	3	2	4	2	5
3	4	3	5	3	6
4	5	4	6	4	7
5	6	5	7	5	8
6	7	6	8	6	9 AM
7	8	7	9 AM	7	10
8	9 AM	8	10	8	11
9 AM	10	9 AM	11	9 AM	12 noon
10	11	10	12 noon	10	1
11	12 noon	11	1	11	2
12 noon	1	12 noon	2	12 noon	3
1	2	1	3	1	4
2	3	2	4	2	5 PM
3	4	3	5 PM	3	6
4	5 PM	4	6	4	7
5 PM	6	5 PM	7	5 PM	8
6	7	6	8	6	9
7	8	7	9	7	10
8	9	8	10	8	11
9	10	9	11	9	12 midnt
10	11	10	12 midnt	10	next day 1 AM
11	12 midnt	11	next day 1 AM	11	2
12 midnt	next day 1 AM	12 midnt	2 AM	12 midnt	3 AM

For information on using these tables, see page 137

138

4 hour difference		5 hour difference		6 hour difference	
Smaller zone number	Larger zone number	Smaller zone number	Larger zone number	Smaller zone number	Larger zone number
1 AM	5 AM	1 AM	6 AM	1 AM	7 AM
2	6	2	7	2	8
3	7	3	8	3	9 AM
4	8	4	9 AM	4	10
5	9 AM	5	10	5	11
6	10	6	11	6	12 noon
7	11	7	12 noon	7	1
8	12 noon	8	1	8	2
9 AM	1	9 AM	2	9 AM	3
10	2	10	3	10	4
11	3	11	4	11	5 PM
12 noon	4	12 noon	5 PM	12 noon	6
1	5 PM	1	6	1	7
2	6	2	7	2	8
3	7	3	8	3	9
4	8	4	9	4	10
5 PM	9	5 PM	10	5 PM	11
6	10	6	11	6	12 midnt
7	11	7	12 midnt	7	next day 1 AM
8	12 midnt	8	next day 1 AM	8	2
9	next day 1 AM	9	2	9	3
10	2	10	3	10	4
11	3	11	4	11	5
12 midnt	4 AM	12 midnt	5 AM	12 midnt	6 AM

7 hour difference		8 hour difference		9 hour difference	
Smaller zone number	Larger zone number	Smaller zone number	Larger zone number	Smaller zone number	Larger zone number
1 AM	8 AM	1 AM	9 AM	1 AM	10 AM
2	9 AM	2	10	2	11
3	10	3	11	3	12 noon
4	11	4	12 noon	4	1
5	12 noon	5	1	5	2
6	1	6	2	6	3
7	2	7	3	7	4
8	3	8	4	8	5 PM
9 AM	4	9 AM	5 PM	9 AM	6
10	5 PM	10	6	10	7
11	6	11	7	11	8
12 noon	7	12 noon	8	12 noon	9
1	8	1	9	1	10
2	9	2	10	2	11
3	10	3	11	3	12 midnt
4	11	4	12 midnt	4	next day 1 AM
5 PM	12 midnt	5 PM	next day 1 AM	5 PM	2
6	next day 1 AM	6	2	6	3
7	2	7	3	7	4
8	3	8	4	8	5
9	4	9	5	9	6
10	5	10	6	10	7
11	6	11	7	11	8
12 midnt	7 AM	12 midnt	8 AM	12 midnt	9 AM

Smaller zone number	Larger zone number	Smaller zone number	Larger zone number	Smaller zone number	Larger zone number
1 AM	**11 AM**	1 AM	**12 noon**	1 AM	**1 PM**
2	**12 noon**	2	**1**	2	**2**
3	**1**	3	**2**	3	**3**
4	**2**	4	**3**	4	**4**
5	**3**	5	**4**	5	**5 PM**
6	**4**	6	**5 PM**	6	6
7	**5 PM**	7	6	7	7
8	6	8	7	8	8
9 AM	7	**9 AM**	8	**9 AM**	9
10	8	**10**	9	**10**	10
11	9	**11**	10	**11**	11
12 noon	10	**12 noon**	11	**12 noon**	12 midnt
1	11	**1**	12 midnt	**1**	next day 1 AM
2	12 midnt	**2**	next day 1 AM	**2**	2
3	next day 1 AM	**3**	2	**3**	3
4	2	**4**	3	**4**	4
5 PM	3	**5 PM**	4	**5 PM**	5
6	4	6	5	6	6
7	5	7	6	7	7
8	6	8	7	8	8
9	7	9	8	9	**9 AM**
10	8	10	**9 AM**	10	**10**
11	**9 AM**	11	**10**	11	**11**
12 midnt	**10 AM**	12 midnt	**11 AM**	12 midnt	**12 noon**

13 hour difference		**14** hour difference		**15** hour difference	
Smaller zone number	Larger zone number	Smaller zone number	Larger zone number	Smaller zone number	Larger zone number
1 AM	2 PM	1 AM	3 PM	1 AM	4 PM
2	3	2	4	2	5 PM
3	4	3	5 PM	3	6
4	5 PM	4	6	4	7
5	6	5	7	5	8
6	7	6	8	6	9
7	8	7	9	7	10
8	9	8	10	8	11
9 AM	10	9 AM	11	9 AM	12 midnt
10	11	10	12 midnt	10	next day 1 AM
11	12 midnt	11	next day 1 AM	11	2
12 noon	next day 1 AM	12 noon	2	12 noon	3
1	2	1	3	1	4
2	3	2	4	2	5
3	4	3	5	3	6
4	5	4	6	4	7
5 PM	6	5 PM	7	5 PM	8
6	7	6	8	6	9 AM
7	8	7	9 AM	7	10
8	9 AM	8	10	8	11
9	10	9	11	9	12 noon
10	11	10	12 noon	10	1
11	12 noon	11	1	11	2
12 midnt	1 PM	12 midnt	2 PM	12 midnt	3 PM

16 hour difference		**17** hour difference		**18** hour difference	
Smaller zone number	Larger zone number	Smaller zone number	Larger zone number	Smaller zone number	Larger zone number
1 AM	5 PM	1 AM	6 PM	1 AM	7 PM
2	6	2	7	2	8
3	7	3	8	3	9
4	8	4	9	4	10
5	9	5	10	5	11
6	10	6	11	6	12 midnt
7	11	7	12 midnt	7	next day 1 AM
8	12 midnt	8	next day 1 AM	8	2
9 AM	next day 1 AM	9 AM	2	9 AM	3
10	2	10	3	10	4
11	3	11	4	11	5
12 noon	4	12 noon	5	12 noon	6
1	5	1	6	1	7
2	6	2	7	2	8
3	7	3	8	3	9 AM
4	8	4	9 AM	4	10
5 PM	9 AM	5 PM	10	5 PM	11
6	10	6	11	6	12 noon
7	11	7	12 noon	7	1
8	12 noon	8	1	8	2
9	1	9	2	9	3
10	2	10	3	10	4
11	3	11	4	11	5 PM
12 midnt	4 PM	12 midnt	5 PM	12 midnt	6 PM

Smaller zone number	Larger zone number	Smaller zone number	Larger zone number	Smaller zone number	Larger zone number
1 AM	8 PM	1 AM	9 PM	1 AM	10 PM
2	9	2	10	2	11
3	10	3	11	3	12 midnt
4	11	4	12 midnt	4	next day 1 AM
5	12 midnt	5	next day 1 AM	5	2
6	next day 1 AM	6	2	6	3
7	2	7	3	7	4
8	3	8	4	8	5
9 AM	4	9 AM	5	9 AM	6
10	5	10	6	10	7
11	6	11	7	11	8
12 noon	7	12 noon	8	12 noon	9 AM
1	8	1	9 AM	1	10
2	9 AM	2	10	2	11
3	10	3	11	3	12 noon
4	11	4	12 noon	4	1
5 PM	12 noon	5 PM	1	5 PM	2
6	1	6	2	6	3
7	2	7	3	7	4
8	3	8	4	8	5 PM
9	4	9	5 PM	9	6
10	5 PM	10	6	10	7
11	6	11	7	11	8
12 midnt	7 PM	12 midnt	8 PM	12 midnt	9 PM

22 hour difference		23 hour difference		24 hour difference	
Smaller zone number	Larger zone number	Smaller zone number	Larger zone number	Smaller zone number	Larger zone number
1 AM	11 PM	1 AM	12 midnt	1 AM	next day 1 AM
2	12 midnt	2	next day 1 AM	2	2
3	next day 1 AM	3	2	3	3
4	2	4	3	4	4
5	3	5	4	5	5
6	4	6	5	6	6
7	5	7	6	7	7
8	6	8	7	8	8
9 AM	7	9 AM	8	9 AM	9 AM
10	8	10	9 AM	10	10
11	9 AM	11	10	11	11
12 noon	10	12 noon	11	12 noon	12 noon
1	11	1	12 noon	1	1
2	12 noon	2	1	2	2
3	1	3	2	3	3
4	2	4	3	4	4
5 PM	3	5 PM	4	5 PM	5 PM
6	4	6	5 PM	6	6
7	5 PM	7	6	7	7
8	6	8	7	8	8
9	7	9	8	9	9
10	8	10	9	10	10
11	9	11	10	11	11
12 midnt	10 PM	12 midnt	11 PM	12 midnt	12 midnt

CORRUPTION INDEX

HOW TO READ THE CHART

The **rank** relates solely to the results drawn from a number of surveys and reflects only the perceptions of businesspeople that participated in these surveys.

The column **1998 CPI Score** relates to perceptions of the degree to which corruption is seen by businesspeople—a perfect 10.00 would be a totally corruption-free country.

Standard Deviation indicates differences in the values of the sources for the 1998 index: the greater the variance, the greater the differences of perceptions of a country among the sources.

The **number of surveys used** had to be at least 3 for a country to be included in the CPI.

Copyright © 1998 Transparency International & Göttingen University

Country Rank	Country	1998 CPI Score	Standard Deviation	Surveys Used
1	Denmark	10.0	0.7	9
2	Finland	9.6	0.5	9
3	Sweden	9.5	0.5	9
4	New Zealand	9.4	0.7	8
5	Iceland	9.3	0.9	6
6	Canada	9.2	0.5	9
7	Singapore	9.1	1.0	10
8	Netherlands	9.0	0.7	9
	Norway	9.0	0.7	9
10	Switzerland	8.9	0.6	10
11	Australia	8.7	0.7	8
	Luxembourg	8.7	0.9	7
	United Kingdom	8.7	0.5	10
14	Ireland	8.2	1.4	10
15	Germany	7.9	0.4	10
16	Hong Kong	7.8	1.1	12
17	Austria	7.5	0.8	9
	United States	7.5	0.9	8
19	Israel	7.1	1.4	9
20	Chile	6.8	0.9	9

Country Rank	Country	1998 CPI Score	Standard Deviation	Surveys Used
21	France	6.7	0.6	9
22	Portugal	6.5	1.0	10
23	Botswana	6.1	2.2	3
	Spain	6.1	1.3	10
25	Japan	5.8	1.6	11
26	Estonia	5.7	0.5	3
27	Costa Rica	5.6	1.6	5
28	Belgium	5.4	1.4	9
29	Malaysia	5.3	0.4	11
	Namibia	5.3	1.0	3
	Taiwan	5.3	0.7	11
32	South Africa	5.2	0.8	10
33	Hungary	5.0	1.2	9
	Mauritius	5.0	0.8	3
	Tunisia	5.0	2.1	3
36	Greece	4.9	1.7	9
37	Czech Republic	4.8	0.8	9
38	Jordan	4.7	1.1	6
39	Italy	4.6	0.8	10
	Poland	4.6	1.6	8
41	Peru	4.5	0.8	6
42	Uruguay	4.3	0.9	3
43	South Korea	4.2	1.2	12
	Zimbabwe	4.2	2.2	6
45	Malawi	4.1	0.6	4
46	Brazil	4.0	0.4	9
47	Belarus	3.9	1.9	3
	Slovak Republic	3.9	1.6	5
49	Jamaica	3.8	0.4	3
50	Morocco	3.7	1.8	3
51	El Salvador	3.6	2.3	3
52	China	3.5	0.7	10
	Zambia	3.5	1.6	4
54	Turkey	3.4	1.0	10
55	Ghana	3.3	1.0	4
	Mexico	3.3	0.6	9
	Philippines	3.3	1.1	10
	Senegal	3.3	0.8	3
59	Ivory Coast	3.1	1.7	4
	Guatemala	3.1	2.5	3

Country Rank	Country	1998 CPI Score	Standard Deviation	Surveys Used
61	Argentina	3.0	0.6	9
	Nicaragua	3.0	2.5	3
	Romania	3.0	1.5	3
	Thailand	3.0	0.7	11
	Yugoslavia	3.0	1.5	3
66	Bulgaria	2.9	2.3	4
	Egypt	2.9	0.6	3
	India	2.9	0.6	12
69	Bolivia	2.8	1.2	4
	Ukraine	2.8	1.6	6
71	Latvia	2.7	1.9	3
	Pakistan	2.7	1.4	3
73	Uganda	2.6	0.8	4
74	Kenya	2.5	0.6	4
	Vietnam	2.5	0.5	6
76	Russia	2.4	0.9	10
77	Ecuador	2.3	1.5	3
	Venezuela	2.3	0.8	9
79	Colombia	2.2	0.8	9
80	Indonesia	2.0	0.9	10
81	Nigeria	1.9	0.5	5
	Tanzania	1.9	1.1	4
83	Honduras	1.7	0.5	3
84	Paraguay	1.5	0.5	3
85	Cameroon	1.4	0.5	4

MARE

MARE TARTA

RICVM

TLAN

MARE

CEANVS

MAR DI

MA

INDIA

TERRA

AVS

TRALIS I

COG

NITA

Meridies

TERRA

BACKGROUND

Getting Through Customs (GTC) is a software, training and research firm for international business travelers. GTC produces the PASSPORT System, the leading online database for international business. PASSPORT contains data on 65 countries in the following areas:

- Business Practices
- Cognitive Styles
- Contacts
- Cultural I.Q. Quizzes
- Cultural Overviews
- Getting Around/Travel
- Historical Chronologies
- Holidays
- Literature
- Medical Information
- Protocol
- Quotations

The data in this book represents just a fraction of the information contained in the PASSPORT System. PASSPORT runs on the Intranets of firms like Arthur Andersen, AT&T, AMR Corporation (SABRE & Travelocity), Deloitte & Touche, DuPont, Ernst & Young, IBM and Lucent Technologies.

PASSPORT is available in html format to transfer directly to corporate and educational Intranets. A free demo of PASSPORT is available on GTC's Website at *http://www.getcustoms.com*.

GTC offers seminars in intercultural communications. These seminars range from a half-day presentation by GTC President Terri Morrison to customized, multi-day workshops conducted by a team. A list of references, content and prices are available upon request.

GTC also employs the authors of several very successful books on international business customs. These books include:

Kiss, Bow or Shake Hands: How to Do Business in 60 Countries by Terri Morrison, Wayne A. Conaway and George A. Borden, Ph.D. (U.S. $19.95, Adams Media, 800-872-5627 or 781-767-8100, ISBN 1-55850-444-3)

Dun & Bradstreet's Guide to Doing Business Around the World by Terri Morrison, Wayne A. Conaway and Joseph J. Douress (U.S. $24.95, Prentice Hall, 800-947-7700 or 515-284-6751, ISBN 0-13-531484-4)

The International Traveler's Guide to Doing Business in Latin America by Terri Morrison and Wayne A. Conaway (U.S. $16.95, Macmillan, 800-428-5331, ISBN 002-86-17-55X)

The International Traveler's Guide to Doing Business in the European Union by Terri Morrison and Wayne A. Conaway (U.S. $16.95, Macmillan, 800-428-5331, ISBN 002-86-17-568)

Bizetiquette.com (tentative title due out in 1999) by Terri Morrison and Wayne A. Conaway (Adams Media, 800-872-5627 or 781-757-8100)

For further information on GTC's PASSPORT Database, Seminars or Books, phone 610-725-1040 or fax 610-725-1074.

E-Mail Address:
TerriMorrison@getcustoms.com

Mailing Address:
638 West Lancaster Avenue, Second Floor, Malvern, PA 19355 USA

Visit our Website:
http://www.getcustoms.com